Dog Lover's Devotional

Print ISBN 978-1-61626-830-5

eBook Editions:
Adobe Digital Edition (.epub) 978-1-62029-080-4
Kindle and MobiPocket Edition (.prc) 978-1-62029-081-1

Cover Photo: Ocean Photography

Published by Barbour Publishing, Inc., P.O. Box 719, Uhrichsville, Ohio 44683, www.barbourbooks.com

Our mission is to publish and distribute inspirational products offering exceptional value and biblical encouragement to the masses.

Member of the
Evangelical Christian
Publishers Association

Printed in the United States of America.

Dog Lover's Devotional

What We Learn about Life from
Our Canine Companions

Katherine A. Douglas

BARBOUR
PUBLISHING

Dedication

*This book is dedicated to
my sister, Lucy Kay Napier,
who has been a passionate animal
lover (horses, dogs, cats, birds, snakes,
goldfish, turtles, and everything in
between—except for her nemesis, raccoons)
for as long as any of us can remember.*

Acknowledgments

*F*riends, relatives, and total strangers have contributed to this book. People at work left me notes; friends living states away sent e-mails. With the tenacity of bulldogs, members of my church family hunted me down with their delightful stories. My mom (and proofreader), Betty Vicary, garnered stories from friends in Ohio, Michigan, and Florida. With the encouragement of my friend Linda, I approached total strangers in restaurants, parks, and airports with one question: Would you tell me about your dog? Men in law enforcement such as Brian Woods and Detective John Greenwood (whom I've never met) and our good neighbors next door have all provided me with some of the stories you will read here. A special thanks to my colleague Chuck Miller for his reflective quotes used throughout this book. Much of the credit for this work goes to Kelly McIntosh at Barbour Publishing. A devotional book for pet lovers was her idea.

To all of these folks and others whom I "hounded" for stories and anecdotes, thank you!

Contents

Preface

Pets have been around since the Creator God started it all. The progenitor of the human race, Adam, was given the high honor of naming every animal in the Garden of Eden. While all animals have value, dogs in particular provide us with entertainment, affection, exercise, and companionship. They make an excellent pair of eyes when our eyes aren't excellent, their noses are superior to any smoke detector we might have, and their ears don't miss the faintest sound. They fiercely protect our young as well as their own. Those of us who have dogs think everyone should have a dog and that there must be something terribly wrong with those who don't.

We teach our dogs tricks: how to roll over, sit, fetch, speak—easy lessons when you think about it. Our dogs teach us the tougher stuff: patience, self-sacrifice, tenacity, gentleness, waiting on God. Dogs can be invaluable teachers when it comes to life's hardest lessons.

Every day we take the time to feed our dogs—or make sure they have food and water available to feed themselves. We care for them because we care about them. The Bible says the "righteous man cares for the needs of his animal" (Proverbs 12:10). That's not at all unlike God, who says we are to cast all our cares and anxieties upon Him, since He cares for us (1 Peter 5:7).

Every account in this collection is true. My prayer is that, as you share the laughter, tears, amazement, and occasional puzzlement of other people about their dogs, you will take to heart the deeper truths behind the stories. Biblical truth surrounds us. The Lord Jesus Christ uses a variety of His creatures to teach us about God and about ourselves. Dinosaurs, donkeys, ants, and dogs are just a smattering of animals He used to teach people of the past—and continues to use as He teaches us today.

So after you've cleaned up the dog's mess one more time or dragged in that twenty-five-pound bag of doggy munchies or combed the obstinate burrs out of the puppy's fur for the third time this week, settle in with your favorite four-legged friend. Catch a dog tale to start off or finish up your day. Some of the Creator's best teachers are the dogs that walk alongside us.

Kathy Douglas

God's Character

What my collie must do he does,
and what he does he must do,
and unwittingly he imitates
the God he can't see
and I follow.

CHUCK MILLER

Poncho

"None has been lost except the one doomed to destruction so that Scripture would be fulfilled."

John 17:12

I'm expecting a call from my dog."

Tim's fork stopped halfway to his mouth. His business associate was from California; he hailed from Ohio. He knew a lot of differences between the two states—and that California usually leads the way in innovation and novelty—but this was beyond anything he had ever dreamed.

"A call from your dog?" he asked.

Nan waved her hand in dismissal. "Not from my dog, of course," she said, "but about him."

Tim felt better already. His food reached its destination before he spoke again. "Is he sick or something? Staying with a family member?"

"No. He's lost."

"Oh. Got someone looking for him?"

"Not exactly. I mean, not by conventional means."

Tim set his fork down. This conversation was doing nothing to improve his appetite. It was taking all his powers of concentration to figure out how one looked for one's dog without looking for one's dog. His colleague rushed on to explain.

"Poncho has a collar that's registered with a company that uses GPS to track missing dogs."

Tim scratched his head. "The Global Positioning System is used to locate your. . .dog?"

Nan wiped her mouth daintily with her napkin. "Sure. Everyone does it. Our area of California is so mountainous and wooded that it would be impossible to find Poncho by conventional means. So this chip emits a signal that can be picked up by a satellite and. . .voilá! The errant dog can be located."

Nan's cell phone rang. She answered it and gave a thumbs-up to Tim.

"The GPS did it! Poncho's been found!"

God never loses sight nor track of people. None are lost to Him unless they willfully choose to walk away. Even Judas Iscariot, who betrayed the Lord Jesus, was given opportunity to repent. When he brought the soldiers to arrest Jesus, the Lord's first word to him was "Friend. . ." (Matthew 26:50). Judas was lost to God's forgiving love because he chose to be. But, like every other man and woman who has ever lived or will ever live, Judas has never been lost from God's sight or consciousness. God has a heart for the lost. He seeks them.

> God never loses sight nor track of people.

Similarly, God has stern words for those who are

irresponsible spiritual shepherds of His people. "You have not brought back the strays or searched for the lost," He said in condemnation of Israel's religious leaders. "I myself will search for my sheep and look after them. . . . I will search for the lost and bring back the strays" (Ezekiel 34:4, 11, 16). And to this the Lord Jesus said and demonstrated that He came "to seek and to save what was lost" (Luke 19:10).

You and I need never question the Lord's commitment and ability to locate the lost—even if we are the lost ones. God's Positioning System is 100 percent accurate 100 percent of the time for 100 percent of His creation.

Mink

For there is one God and one mediator between God and men,
the man Christ Jesus.

1 Timothy 2:5

She picked up the telephone and dialed 911. She had awakened suddenly at 1:00 a.m. Her husband, a victim of Alzheimer's disease, was gone. A quick, panicked search about the house proved futile.

The sheriff's department contacted the local volunteer fire department. Firefighters arrived and started combing the area, but to no avail. Finally, someone thought to enlist the help of a police dog.

In law enforcement circles, Mink, a German shepherd, is called a dual-purpose dog, working in both narcotics and on patrol for tracking, criminal apprehension, and police protection. Mink is trained to find illegal drugs and people. When Mink and his sidekick first joined the search, things did not go well. Mink kept picking up trails that had been made by the searching firefighters. The small subdivision was bound by an interstate toll road, a river, and a marsh. Once Mink was allowed to "free scan," he picked up another trail. Dog and man were off in the middle of the night with Mink in the lead.

But long minutes became an hour. Mink's partner

began to feel frustrated. They had been through more terrain than one elderly man could have possibly ventured through in the dark! The temperature continued to plummet. Mink kept tracking farther from the man's home. They went through the marsh and ended up in another small subdivision. Mink's trainer was ready to quit, thinking Mink was on the wrong trail. Suddenly Mink stopped. There lay the man on the ground, almost frozen but still alive. Mink had found him!

Mink, as it turned out, was the right "man" for the job.

In wonderful detail the writer of Hebrews goes to great lengths to show us why Jesus Christ alone was and is the right man to bring salvation to the world. Christ is presented as being better than the angels, though

> **God sent Jesus— the right man for the right job at the right time.**

they are described as "winds. . .flames of fire" (Hebrews 1:7). Jesus is better than Moses. Moses was faithful as a servant in God's house, but Christ is faithful as a Son in charge of the entire household (3:1–6). The Lord Christ is superior to the Aaronic priesthood "on the basis of the power of an indestructible life" (7:16). Jesus—and Jesus alone—did for us what no other could do. "At just the right time, when we were still powerless, Christ died for the ungodly" (Romans 5:6). God sent Jesus—the right man for the right job at the right time.

A large contingent of rescue-minded people were powerless to rescue one victim. Only Mink was able to deliver the wanderer from imminent physical death. So, too, only Jesus stands between us and eternal death. Are you trusting in Jesus Christ alone today as your Savior? He alone is the way to God. "Salvation is found in no one else, for there is no other name under heaven given to men by which we must be saved" (Acts 4:12).

Cal

You are my hiding place;
you will protect me from trouble.
PSALM 32:7

Cal, a Jack Russell terrier, may look like something of a sluggard. During summer's hot days he likes to pass the time of day in the family pool. Cal doesn't get right into the pool. He prefers to spend some time sunbathing first. He waits patiently until the kids' inflatable alligator toy floats over to the side of the pool where he waits. Then, in one quick leap, he jumps onto the alligator and spreads himself out prone over the plastic toy. There he contentedly naps until he purposely slips off his personal flotation device. He swims back to the edge of the pool, shakes himself dry, and gets a drink of fresh water. He's had his time in the sun to his satisfaction.

To see Cal lounging about in such a manner might mislead one into thinking Cal is not an action dog. But appearances can be deceiving. Cal can be catapulted into aggressive action from his spot on the alligator. All it takes is what he perceives to be a physical threat to Jackie and Lisa, his teenage owners. Instantly Cal becomes attack dog extraordinaire.

John, the girls' dad, loves to tease his daughters with an

occasional good tickling. Recently John and his girls got into some rowdy horseplay. When the tickling started, so did the girls' screaming. Cal, not knowing screams due to tickling are different from screams due to trouble, sprang to the rescue.

Papa let go a scream himself when Cal jumped up, teeth bared, to attach himself to John's backside!

"In the last days scoffers will come. . . . They will say, 'Where is this "coming" he promised? Ever since our fathers died, everything goes on as it has since the beginning of creation'" (2 Peter 3:3–4).

"He who watches over Israel will neither slumber nor sleep" (Psalm 121:4).

"The Lord is not slow in keeping his promise, as some understand slowness" (2 Peter 3:9).

"How long, Sovereign Lord, holy and true, until you judge the inhabitants of the earth and avenge our blood?" (Revelation 6:10).

To saints and sinners alike, in the past, in the present, and yet in the future, it seems that God is not active in human affairs. Some think that God, like Cal, is simply floating about somewhere outside the cosmos, indifferent to the ebb and flow of human life. Some are not scoffers, but they are completely ignorant of God and His patience with people. Some who "suffer for righteousness' sake" (1 Peter 3:14 kjv) wonder if the Lord is going to tarry indefinitely.

Scripture assures us time and again that our God is active among us. "For the Lord your God moves about in your camp to protect you" (Deuteronomy 23:14). The Lord said, "Where two or three come together in my name, there am I with them" (Matthew 18:20). Someday the "Lord Almighty will come down to do battle" (Isaiah 31:4).

> God is active among us. His unseen footprints are all around us.

God is active among us. His unseen footprints are all around us.

Parker

*"If a man owns a hundred sheep, and one of them
wanders away, will he not leave the ninety-nine on the hills
and go to look for the one that wandered off?
And if he finds it. . .he is happier about that one sheep
than about the ninety-nine that did not wander off."*

MATTHEW 18:12–13

*S*amantha, not yet three years old, was heartbroken. Her
dog, Parker (Samantha pronounces it "Pow-kuh"), got
spooked in a bad thunderstorm while the family was gone.
Terrified, Parker had run off. Samantha's parents, Lara and
Eric, instituted a neighborhood search to find him. As they
walked along the streets, they called for Parker repeatedly.
At the end of the first day, they had not found him.

Samantha had one question: "Is Pow-kuh home yet?"

Day two started the way day one ended. "Is Pow-kuh
home yet?" Samantha's tears weren't lagging far behind her
quivering lip.

Samantha's parents again combed the neighborhood,
widening their search. At one house, a couple, busy doing
lawn work, shook their heads.

"We don't live around here," they said. "We're just
taking care of our parents' lawn. Sorry we can't be of any
help."

At the end of two days, Eric and Lara had all but given up. Perhaps Parker had been stolen.

Later that evening, the telephone rang. The couple who had been working in their parents' yard were calling.

"You're not going to believe this," the man said, "but we came home, and we think your dog is in our yard!"

A short time later, Samantha made a beeline for the exhausted-looking, weary dog that sat on the strangers' porch. "Pow-kuh! Pow-kuh!" After his ordeal, Parker could only perk up his ears and give his tail a few weak wags. But it was enough for Samantha.

The lost was found!

Just as Parker is precious to his young mistress, so every lost sinner is important to God. The Lord Jesus Christ used numerous parables to teach us the importance of each individual in the eyes of the Creator. The lost sheep, the lost coin, and the lost son are all word pictures given in Luke 15 to show us the inestimable value of every man, woman, boy, and girl to the Lord who made them.

> Jesus Christ went beyond using parables to describe God's love for people.

Jesus Christ went beyond using parables to describe God's love for people. He demonstrated it. He met with people in groups and enjoyed their company one-on-one. Indignant, the upstanding religious people of His day condemned the Lord by muttering, "This man welcomes sinners and eats with them" (Luke 15:2). The Lord sought out one cheating tax collector and was delighted when the man repented (19:1–10). The Lord sailed over the sea to touch and heal one man with many demons (Mark 5:1–21). God is focused on people—one at a time.

Like Samantha's parents, committed to finding one lost dog, so the Lord seeks lost people. We are valuable—of singular, inestimable worth—to God.

Packwood and Neola

For this God is our God for ever and ever;
he will be our guide even to the end.

PSALM 48:14

GUIDE DOG IN TRAINING.

That's what the canvas coats over each of the two young yellow Labradors read. The young dogs walked obediently beside the two trainers, content to take their places under the table at the restaurant.

Don and Jeanne have been training dogs for the blind for many years. Trainers receive their dogs when the puppies are eight weeks old. The trainers then have their adopted puppy-in-training for one year. Packwood, so light in color that he almost looks golden white, and Neola, a darker blond Lab, are in the middle of their preprofessional training. Their trainers will be responsible for housebreaking the two dogs and teaching them socialization skills. Both humans love the work, though they admit it's hard when the time comes to send their dogs off for their professional training. Labrador retrievers, golden retrievers, German shepherds, and mixes of the three breeds are all used as guide dogs in Don and Jeanne's organization.

"We get very attached to our dogs," Jeanne admits,

"but we have a new puppy in our arms almost before our current one is out the door."

Once the dogs are sent away to school, their first trainers are given weekly updates on the dogs' progress. Of all the dogs that enter training, only about 50 percent will complete it. Labradors are most likely to succeed, but German shepherds continue to be student guide dogs.

"Most people are afraid of shepherds," Helen, another trainer, says. "People who are blind feel the additional benefit of protection with the more imposing shepherds. Sighted people will quickly reach to pet a Lab or a golden retriever. They aren't so quick to pat a shepherd on the head."

> God is our faithful guide in life.

"We try to teach sighted people not to touch the dogs without asking permission first," say the trainers. All three humans enjoy their work and enjoy their dogs.

And the dogs? When Neola's trainer came into the room after parking the car, it was clear that Neola only had eyes for her.

God is our faithful guide in life. He not only guides us as individuals, but He guides "the nations of the earth" (Psalm 67:4). Asaph praised God when he said, "You guide me with your counsel" (73:24), and the Lord Jesus promised us that the Holy Spirit guides us "into all truth" (John 16:13).

There can be no regret or sorrow when people such as

Don, Jeanne, and Helen see the results of their training and love. Trainers are always invited to the graduation ceremony—the joining of one of their dogs to its lifetime partner.

"The LORD will guide you always," the Word promises us (Isaiah 58:11). Just as people who are blind bond with their new companions, we can depend on God's faithful guidance today and every day even though we cannot see Him beside us.

Buffy

"I give [my sheep] eternal life. . .
no one can snatch them out of my hand. . .
[or] my Father's hand."

JOHN 10:28–29

MaryBeth and her husband had just moved to the country when a young blond cocker spaniel came scraping at the front door. MaryBeth tried to ignore her at first, but the little cocker was nothing if not persistent.

"I am not opening this door," MaryBeth said through the closed front door.

The dog went around to MaryBeth's back door. There MaryBeth could see her completely: eager, bright-eyed, barking, and. . .shivering.

MaryBeth sighed and brought the little dog into her garage where she was warmed, fed, and watered. Then MaryBeth started making telephone calls to her neighbors.

"Did you lose a blond cocker spaniel?" was her question.

Every neighbor laughed at her query. "You're in the country now, honey. That dog is yours!"

"But I don't want a dog!"

"Finders, keepers! People drop innocent animals out

in the middle of nowhere all the time. You won't find any owner. That dog is yours to keep."

Everyone gave her the same response. MaryBeth went canvassing from house to house. More of the same. A snicker, a shake of the head, and a shrugged that-dog-is-yours platitude.

MaryBeth ran ads; she placed a sign in her yard; she distributed flyers. No inquiries.

Just to call her something, MaryBeth started calling the dog "Buffy" in keeping with her coloring. She patted Buffy on the head in sympathy. Days passed; still no response to her search efforts. Maybe her neighbors were right.

Two weeks went by.

MaryBeth's husband came home from work late one afternoon, a look of triumph on his face.

"Hey! I found a guy at work who's got a big fenced yard. He'll take the dog!"

MaryBeth quickly scooped up Buffy and wrapped her arms defensively around her. "You're not taking my dog anywhere!"

Ownership. Possession. We will fight for what we love the most.

God is like that with us. Unlike Buffy, we do not come to God seeking His love. He draws and woos us. "You did not choose me, but I chose you," He says (John 15:16). His love is a properly placed, jealous love because He alone is God our Maker. He makes no apologies for his possessiveness. "Do not worship any other god," He says, "for the LORD, whose name is Jealous, is a jealous God" (Exodus 34:14).

The Lord's right hand holds us fast, and once we are under His care, His grip on us is unbreakable. He "will keep your foot from being snared" (Proverbs 3:26). From Genesis to Revelation, our holy, jealous, loving God is in the business of keeping us.

> His love is a properly placed, jealous love because He alone is God our Maker.

Like MaryBeth clinging to her beloved Buffy, no matter what comes, the Lord will never let us go.

Discouragement and Encouragement

The countenance of my collie's whole being can be transported from despair to elation at the sound of a single word—any of several will do—from his god alone; I wish my trust had such a vocabulary and my vocabulary such a trust.

CHUCK MILLER

Mattie

And what does the LORD require of you?
To act justly and to love mercy and to walk humbly with your God.

MICAH 6:8

*T*ake yourself for a walk."

Mattie is a chocolate Labrador who enjoys taking walks with her master, Marty. He enjoys these walks, too, but sometimes Mattie's timing doesn't match Marty's. On one particular sunny spring day, Marty and his wife went to their son's ball game along with some other family members. Mattie went, but baseball isn't what she considers fun. After an inning or two, she had had enough of the game. She started pestering Marty to take her for a walk.

Marty interrupted his conversation with his sister. He looked down at the whimpering nuisance. Both command and permission were given in one sentence.

"Take yourself for a walk."

Marty's sister couldn't believe what she saw next. Mattie picked up the distal end of the leash in her mouth. She merrily trotted off to take a walk around the more interesting ballpark grounds. Marty's sister looked back at her brother in disbelief.

"Is she really. . . ?"

He waved off her question and turned his attention

back to the game. "She does it all the time. If I can't take her for a walk, she does it herself."

Marty's sister looked behind her one more time. There was Mattie, prancing jauntily about the grounds, her leash snugly—and somewhat smugly—clamped between her teeth. She'd gotten her way and her walk. She did not need a human on the other end of her leash to get her daily exercise. She could do it by herself.

From our beginning, God has desired that we walk both *with* Him and *like* Him. Our walk has to do with how we live our lives every day. We're admonished to "be very careful. . . how [we] live" (Ephesians 5:15). In the King James Version, those words read, "See then that ye walk circumspectly." God has not and does not keep us on a leash, but His expectation is that we walk—that we live—as if He were physically beside us. He does not want us to walk independently of Him. He made that clear to the nation of Israel and to all who name Christ as Savior.

> From our beginning, God has desired that we walk both *with* Him and *like* Him.

"Do two walk together unless they have agreed to do so?" is the rhetorical question put to us by the prophet Amos (Amos 3:3). To walk humbly with our God is to be in agreement with Him and His holy character. God will not send us off on our own for a walk. He is right beside us, encouraging us with these words: "This is the way; walk in it" (Isaiah 30:21).

Love is God's leash; His Spirit, our companion.

Zach

"How I long for the months gone by, for the days when God watched over me, when his lamp shone upon my head and by his light I walked through darkness!"

JOB 29:2–3

Zach, a frisky peekapoo, had a good life. He was the pride and joy of his new owner, Loylene, and had to share her attention only with Beauregard, the family feline. Originally, Zach was to be a gift to Loylene's mom, but while she was on a protracted vacation, Zach bonded with Loylene. By the time an additional six months had passed (miles separated Zach from his new home), there was no parting Zach and Loylene.

Life was good until Zach had surgery. The procedure went smoothly; there was only one problem. Zach always slept on his tummy, his back legs stretched out behind him. With his fresh incision, Zach could no longer sleep prone. He was miserable.

Zach turned this way and that, trying to get comfortable. He couldn't sleep standing up; he couldn't sleep sitting up. What was a dog to do? Finally, he flopped down awkwardly on his side, his back legs stretched out beside him instead of behind him. There was nothing else to be done in his misery.

Zach heaved a big, heavy sigh.

Misery. Whether it's physical, emotional, or spiritual misery, when it comes, life loses its luster. Throughout the book that bears his name, Job laments his great losses. He lost everything—except for his whining wife. Job was on the brink of losing his faith as well. Initially he had the stamina to reply to his wife, "Shall we accept good from God, and not trouble?" (Job 2:10). But one chapter later, Job was wallowing in his misery. "What I dreaded has happened to me" (3:25).

Job isn't the only who had trouble keeping his chin up when circumstances soured. Elijah, through whom God demonstrated His power unequivocally, cried to God in his misery. "I have been very zealous for the LORD God Almighty," he said. "I am the only one left, and now they are trying to kill me too" (1 Kings 19:14).

Where is God when it hurts—whatever "it" is?

God—who does not lie—says He is with us. "I live in a high and holy place, but also with him who is contrite and lowly in spirit" (Isaiah 57:15). "And surely I am with you always" (Matthew 28:20). "For he has not despised or disdained the suffering of the afflicted one; he has not hidden his face from him but has listened to his cry for help" (Psalm 22:24).

> Out of your suffering God can—and will—bring glory.

If you're in the midst of suffering today, be assured you are not alone. He is with you. Out of your suffering God can—and will—bring glory. Your "present sufferings are not worth comparing with the glory that will be revealed" in you (Romans 8:18).

Pete

Pete, a beefy, bulky American bulldog, is an ominous presence to those who don't know him. The only thing scarier than his massive frame is his ugly face. Despite his considerable size, Pete has energy to spare. He loves to run and roughhouse with his owner, Mike. When Mike is ready for some serious wrestling, Pete is more than ready. There's nothing like a good wrestling match as far as Pete is concerned.

But for others, there are some concerns. Mike and his wife, Shelly, have two toddlers, Jared and Olivia, and a newborn baby, Jake. The children are dwarfed by their canine big brother. The toddlers love to play, too, but unlike their father, they are clearly no match for the husky bulldog. Everyone understands that—except (perhaps) Jared and Olivia.

The first time Olivia set her sights on something out of her reach, she used Pete as her stepping stool. One moment she was toddling across the floor. The next moment she was balancing herself on Pete's fur-covered spine. With a collective gasp, everyone in the room jumped up to whisk Olivia off Pete's back before the big bulldog turned on her.

Pete and Olivia were both stunned. Olivia had no idea why she suddenly found herself dangling in midair above Pete. Pete was puzzled by all the leaping adults around them. He knew Olivia wasn't about to wrestle with him. He was quite content to serve as her step stool.

Let the little lady stomp up (and down, if she wants) his spine! He was dog enough to provide her with any vantage point she needed!

High-energy Pete calmly looked around the room at everyone. He never flinched.

He has been Olivia's trusted, true, rock-solid stepping-stone ever since.

"The LORD will keep you from all harm—he will watch over your life," declared the psalmist (Psalm 121:7). In Romans we're told "that in all things God works for the good of those who love him" (Romans 8:28). In times of peril, it may appear that God is just waiting to snap at us for a misstep or misdeed. But that is not the character of our God.

Even when the Israelites were in exile, God reassured them. " 'For I know the plans I have for you,' declares the LORD, 'plans to prosper you and not to harm you, plans to give you hope and a future' " (Jeremiah 29:11). God no more intended harm for his people then than He does now. The stepping-stones He provides along the way may appear to be unsteady rocks at best—unpredictable snares at worst—but God knows what

He's about. He will not inadvertently or accidentally harm His own. "The Lord knows those who are his" (2 Timothy 2:19). God is our trustworthy rock.

Taking an unsure step today? Tackling a new project unlike anything in your past? Climbing new heights that look fraught with peril? Pray with the psalmist:

> God is our trustworthy rock.

"Lead me to the rock that is higher than I" (Psalm 61:2).

Boomer

*Now the serpent was more crafty than any of
the wild animals the Lord God had made.*

GENESIS 3:1

Larry, a fiftysomething retired police officer, came
hobbling home after an afternoon at his daughter's.
His wife looked at him, puzzled. He went to get some
pain relievers, and she followed him, waiting to hear the
explanation for his obvious discomfort.

"We were playing some touch football," he said.
"Boomer took me out like a linebacker! He came at me
from the side and knocked my legs out from under me.
I went down like a ton of bricks!"

His wife was just about to ask why Boomer,
whomever he was, tackled her husband during a game
of touch football, when Larry continued. "But I fared
better than Fred. Boomer took a good-sized bite out of
his leg!"

Larry downed the pain relievers with his glass of
water. His wife followed him back into the living room.

"Who's this Boomer guy? And why is he tackling and
biting people?" she asked.

"Boomer! Boomer is Greg's dog."

"Ahh!"

Boomer is a shepherd-Lab mix who's as muscular and strong as his name implies. He loves to run but was inconspicuously watching the game from the sidelines. Then the ball was kicked. Larry caught it. He started running up the field with it.

Boomer saw the kick, saw the catch, saw the run. He went after the prize! He came out of nowhere, blindsided Larry, and dove at the receiver's legs. Lean muscle powered every one of his eighty pounds.

Sharp teeth were all Boomer needed to make his mark on Fred.

> When the enemy comes upon you today, remember that the Lord gives us the wherewithal to resist him.

It's hard to say who had the greater injury—Larry, with grass in his teeth and mud on his face, or Fred, with some precise canine indentations in his calf.

Our "enemy the devil prowls around like a roaring lion looking for someone to devour" (1 Peter 5:8). Sometimes the evil one exercises even greater stealth. He "masquerades as an angel of light" (2 Corinthians 11:14). Whether he appears to be an angel or acts like a lion, Satan is "the dragon, that ancient serpent, who is the devil" (Revelation 20:2), and his demise is sure. His fall will be complete. We need to be wary of him, to be on our guard and to be wise, but God is the only One we need fear.

When the enemy comes upon you today, remember that the Lord gives us the wherewithal to resist him. "Call upon me in the day of trouble" (Psalm 50:15), the Lord says. When we "are tempted, he will also provide a way out so that [we] can stand up under it" (1 Corinthians 10:13).

Satan's teeth may be sharper than Boomer's, but he cannot devour those in God's protective hand, and he cannot trip those who stand firm in their faith.

Boots

*The LORD said to Satan, "Very well, then,
everything he has is in your hands,
but on the man himself do not lay a finger."*
JOB 1:12

*B*oots is the consummate toddler babysitter.

Fawn-colored with a black face, a white star on his forehead, and four white paws, Boots the boxer is a no-nonsense sitter. In spite of his muscular ninety pounds, Boots is as gentle with his three-year-old charge, Doug, as a nanny. Doug's mom has seen her son use Boots's ears for teething rings. Boots grimaces, but he doesn't bite, snap, yelp, or run away. Boots loves Doug; he would never do a thing to harm him. But, being a toddler, Doug has been given limits. Sometimes Boots must remind Doug of those limits.

One sunny afternoon, Doug's mother was watching her son covertly to see what he would do in their fenced backyard. Doug was outside with Boots. The toddler stayed busy in his yard for a while. Then he saw something beyond the fence that appealed to him: freedom from restraint. With impressive concentration and determination, Doug climbed up and over the fence.

Boots looked once at Doug's mother and sprang into

action. He leaped over the fence in one bound and sprinted after Doug, who was merrily toddling toward the street. Boots grabbed the seat of little Doug's pants, plopping him down to a sitting position. Doug, who was no match for the big boxer, found himself anchored to the spot until his mother came and returned him to the backyard again.

Three times that day Doug determinedly climbed the fence. Three times Boots vaulted the same fence. Three times Boots resolutely grabbed Doug by his drawers and sat him down. Boots was out to teach Doug his limits—with all the determination of a strong-willed toddler.

God never explains completely to us why bad things happen to good people. When Satan challenged God a second time with regard to Job, God recanted—or so it may seem to us—by allowing the evil one to inflict terrible physical suffering upon Job (Job 2:6). Sometimes we may fear that there is no limit to the evil that may befall us, but the Lord assures us that He is the "blessed controller of all things" (1 Timothy 6:15 PHILLIPS). God alone is "far above all rule and authority, power and dominion, and every title that can be given" (Ephesians 1:21).

> God never explains completely to us why bad things happen to good people.

Satan declared that he would make himself equal with God. He set out to break the limits put on him by the Maker of all. "I will. . ." was his redundant declaration as he sought to usurp the power and place that are God's alone (see Isaiah 14:12–14). God expelled Satan "from among the fiery stones" (Ezekiel 28:16) and someday will finally consign him to the eternal fire that has been prepared for him.

Don't despair if the enemy appears to be getting the upper hand in your life or in the world at large. Like Boots holding on to Doug's britches, God is in control.

Chipper

"But the cowardly, the unbelieving, the vile,
the murderers, the sexually immoral,
those who practice magic arts,
the idolaters and all liars—their place
will be in the fiery lake of burning sulfur."

REVELATION 21:8

Chipper has no history of being a vicious or unpredictable dog. Occasionally he digs his way out of the yard, though. Once he flattens himself out enough, he scoots under the fence, runs around to the front of the house, and. . .sits down in the driveway. Chipper stays there until a family member discovers him and herds him into the house or backyard. Chipper's curiosity is not enough to drive him beyond the boundaries of his own yard.

One fall, ten-year-old Luke suited up for football practice. His buddies, in similar American male autumn regalia, came over to get him. Chipper took one look at the boys who had been transformed into burly pigskin players and cowered in terror.

A Labrador afraid of ten-year-olds in football uniforms? A dog afraid to go outside his yard? Luke and his family couldn't believe their Chipper was a coward.

Perhaps these two instances were just flukes. But the day came for Chipper's mettle to be put to the test.

Chipper had gotten out of the backyard again. Luke came out of the house to corral his dog. That's when Luke saw the postal carrier. Their unsuspecting, preoccupied mail carrier was approaching their house. There sat Chipper on the driveway, between Luke and the stranger. Chipper's eyes focused on the advancing postal carrier.

What would happen? Would Chipper pick today to be Luke's champion and protector? Would Chipper run toward the stranger and bite him? Would the postal employee zap Chipper with his hot pepper spray? Could Luke somehow come between the postal carrier and the black Lab before there was an altercation? Luke held his breath. Sure enough, Chipper sprang into action!

He ran—and hid—behind Luke's legs.

As Jesus Christ, King of Kings and Lord of Lords, sits on His throne before the apostle John, He tells His beloved disciple that the Holy City has been prepared for those who overcome. Then He gives John a list of those for whom it is not prepared. First on the list of heinous sins is not murder, idolatry, or sexual immorality, but cowardice (Revelation 21:8). The Greek word here is not the one commonly used in the New Testament for fear (*phóbos* and its derivations), but *deilós*—a derivative of the word for cowardice and timidity.

Jesus' use of this word occurs once during His earthly ministry. He walked on the storm-tossed sea and rebuked the wind and quieted the waves. Then He rebuked

> For the Lord Jesus Christ, faith is never a crutch. Our faith, our trust in Him, is what gives us boldness.

His disciples for their fear (cowardice). "Why are you so afraid?" He asked His men. "Do you still have no faith?" (Mark 4:40). For the Lord Jesus Christ, faith is never a crutch. Our faith, our trust in Him, is what gives us boldness. We don't have to live like Chipper the Chicken.

Jake

Now to him who is able to do immeasurably more than all we ask or imagine, according to his power that is at work within us, to him be glory!
EPHESIANS 3:20–21

One of the most popular names for dogs in the United States is Jake. With a masculine name like Jake, we might picture a big, burly boxer. But this Jake is a mature dog who tips the scales at six pounds after a full meal. Jake is a Yorkie with more energy in his tiny frame than a ten-year-old boy on the soccer field. Jake is a dynamo when it comes time for his favorite activity, a neighborhood walk.

Walk! Even if Linda, his owner, tries to outsmart Jake by spelling w-a-l-k, he knows something's up. He hangs a little closer, he meanders over to where his leash hangs, or his ears stand up a bit higher. Jake may even emit a throaty squeak or whine of impatience.

Once Linda reaches for that leash, Jake is up in the air, dancing around the kitchen floor, barking, whining, and salivating uncontrollably. There's no stopping the explosion of excitement once that "walk" word has hit the air and Linda has taken down the leash. Jake is out of control. Fastening the leash to his collar is no small feat, even for a woman twenty times his size. Once the leash is on, out the back door they go!

Zrrrrrrrrrp!

That leash is as taut as a high wire. It's walk time! If dogs could fly, Jake would be airborne as soon as he leaves the back porch. He is energized from nose to tail. He runs from tree to bush to leaf. Everything warrants a cursory inspection, and nothing is ignored. This little dog is dynamite when it comes to his walk. He is empowered—energized—by this daily delight called his walk.

When God tells us in Ephesians that He operates "according to his power that is at work within us," He's using words that come right out of a powder keg. The Greek word for "power" in this passage is *dynamis;* the word for "at work" is *energos.* We get our English words *dynamite* and *energy* or *energize* from these words.

Do you have Jake days: days—or moments—when you've been energized by the truth that God is able to do immeasurably more than we ask or imagine? Isn't it a marvel that the God of the universe is at work energizing us? Perhaps you can't run or walk or bark wildly about the power at work in you, but you can strain at the leash of the downward pull of the cares of this life. Prayerfully look to him who tells us to "fix our eyes on Jesus" (Hebrews 12:2).

> Isn't it a marvel that the God of the universe is at work energizing us?

Be like energized, dynamic Jake and run in your spirit! The Master is ready for you to pull taut the leash in His loving hand.

Walking the Talk

I can see all of God's responses to my
prayers in my responses to my collie:
Yes; No; Wait;
Let's play; Come; Stay;
Get away from that; Drop it!
How about a treat?
How about a walk?

CHUCK MILLER

Solomon and Pooch

*"Come, let us. . .find out
who is responsible for this calamity."*
JONAH 1:7

*S*olomon, a beautiful Siberian husky with pale-blue eyes, had two great loves in life. One was running. On his owners' five-acre lot, Solomon could run to his heart's content. Solomon's other love was his running buddy, Pooch. Pooch was part Saint Bernard and part. . .something else, from which he inherited skinny legs disproportionate to his burly body.

Because Solomon wasn't street-smart, his owner, Jackie, had her huge backyard installed with invisible fencing for Solomon's safekeeping. Solomon's collar gave him a slight shock if he tried to go outside the confines of his yard. Pooch, who was street savvy and had no such collar or restrictions, came over daily to play with Solomon.

Pooch would occasionally dare Solomon to cross the line and run free with him. Sporadically, Solomon would do it. He would tuck his neck in, run through the invisible barrier, and never look back. Jackie would come home from work, and there would be Solomon, waiting just outside the invisible fence to get back in. (Escape was worth the shock, but not so the return.)

Pooch enticed Solomon out of his yard one time too many.

After a full night of running the countryside, Pooch and Solomon returned from their escapade early in the morning. Pooch looked before he crossed the street. Solomon did not. He was killed instantly by a passing motorist.

For three days, Pooch never came to Jackie's house. When he finally did, he came with his head hung low and his eyes downcast. He trudged to the rear of the property where Jackie and her husband had buried Solomon.

Every day for weeks, Pooch lay at the grave of his dead friend.

Responsibility. We teach it to our children. We feel the weight of it in one form or another every day. There's no escaping its rewards or its consequences—even if you're a dog.

When God gave Jonah specific instructions to preach to a city of wicked people, Jonah got aboard a ship going in the opposite direction. God was out to save the Ninevites from their own self-destruction. He wouldn't take no for an answer.

The sailors with Jonah knew he was running from God. They knew—and Jonah knew—that the great storm came because of Jonah's disobedience. "I know that it is my fault that this great storm has come upon you," Jonah admitted. He told the sailors that throwing him into the sea would save them. To their credit, these men tried everything else before finally throwing Jonah—the storm's responsible party—into the sea (Jonah 1).

People have come up with theories as complex as evolution and excuses as simplistic as "I didn't know" to duck their responsibilities, but the Bible tells us that everyone is accountable to God (Romans 14:12).

> How much more is God thrilled with us when we do the right thing.

Thrilled when your young ones act responsibly? How much more is God thrilled with us when we do the right thing.

Duchess One

All the believers were one in heart and mind.
No one claimed that any of his possessions
was his own, but they shared everything they had.

ACTS 4:32

Many years ago, Gaynell, her husband, and their two growing boys had a dog named Duchess, a red cocker. Being the family pet was not Duchess's idea, however. She wanted to be Gaynell's pet exclusively. More than that, Duchess wanted Gaynell to be exclusively hers.

This would not have been a problem if Gaynell ever had a burglar in the house (but she never did). It was a small problem when the meter reader came. The gas man, as he used to be called, would come every month, banging on the back door, simultaneously yelling, "Gas man!" He would be allowed in by the lady of the house (few married women with children worked outside the home back then), tip his hat, run down to the basement to get a reading, and be gone in a snap of the fingers—except at Gaynell's house with Duchess standing by. No one got past Duchess—least of all the gas man. Gaynell had to corral Duchess in a room so the meter could be read. One problem was solved—but there was another.

The family dog, who refused to be the family dog, restricted her master's movement around the house. When

Gaynell's husband worked second shift, he would come home—but not be allowed in his own room. If he worked days and got up during the night, Duchess would not allow him to go back to bed. Gaynell would then have to get up and go into another room while her husband went back to bed. This was the only way Gaynell's husband could get into their room. He had to be there first. Duchess refused to share her mistress with anyone.

If there is one word any two-year-old child hates more than *no*, it's *share*. Few of us, even as adults, want to share what is dearest to us. We share our leftovers and our second bests, but sharing our prized possessions is tough.

For the early Jerusalem church, sharing was a beautiful practice. Though the church was under persecution, "there were no needy persons among them" (Acts 4:34). One man sold a parcel of land and donated all the money to the Jerusalem church leaders.

Sharing must come from the heart. If it is practiced under compulsion or for show, the results can be disastrous. Ananias and Sapphira made a pretense of generously sharing and died for their duplicity (Acts 5:1–11). In the church at Corinth, sharing meals became a sham (1 Corinthians 11:17–22). The apostle Paul lamented, "Not one church shared with me in the matter of giving and receiving"—except the Philippian church (Philippians 4:15).

> **Sharing must come from the heart.**

Sharing involves sacrifice, but God desires it. "And do not forget to do good and to share with others, for with such sacrifices God is pleased" (Hebrews 13:16).

Cookie

*"If someone forces you to go one mile,
go with him two miles."*

Matthew 5:41

Cookie, a mutt of uncertain ancestry, is a ballplayer. If
she had her way, she would play ball every waking hour of
every day. She wears Bill out with her constant chasing after
and retrieving the ball. When the two of them are outside
together, Bill plays ball with Cookie for a while. Bill has a
yard to maintain, however, and there's only so much time
to play ball. Soon Cookie must sit, watching Bill cut grass.

Cookie watched this grass-cutting ritual for a while.
She sat in the grass, her tail wagging slowly from side to
side. Her ball beside her, Cookie knew the lawn mower
always meant the game was over. But Cookie continued to
watch. And learn. She watched Bill mow—back and forth,
back and forth. Then, a spark of genius!

Cookie picked up the ball, trotted over, and plopped
the ball right in front of the lawn mower. Bill picked it up
and threw it out of the way. Cookie ran after her ball and
brought it back to Bill, dropping it in the long grass again.
When Bill got to it, he reached down and threw the ball
a little farther. Cookie bounded after it, retrieving it once
again. Scampering back jauntily, she dropped it in front

of the approaching lawn mower. Bill grumbled, picked up the ball, and threw it yet again. Cookie merrily took off to retrieve it. She was smug.

The game was going into extra innings!

Our expression "going the extra mile" comes from Matthew 5:41: "If someone forces you to go one mile, go with him two miles." Originally the word *force* came from Persia. Couriers for the postal service had the right to press anyone into service to get the mail delivered. Going the extra mile had nothing to do with volunteerism—it was compulsion, pure and simple.

> God wants us to do the unexpected— the godly thing.

Throughout Matthew 5, Jesus says, "You have heard that it was said...," then continues with, "But I tell you..." There are two ways to live: the human way and God's way. The Lord frequently contrasts the two. He tells us to choose God's way of doing things.

God wants us to do the unexpected—the godly thing. Our Lord wants us to be people of fidelity in deed and in thought. He doesn't want us to qualify our words but to be forthright. He wants us to go beyond doing what we are compelled to do. What He asks is no small thing; we are to "be perfect, therefore, as [our] heavenly Father is perfect" (Matthew 5:48).

Are you like Bill, needing to be coerced into a game of ball? Or will you take the initiative today, not doing what most do but rather doing what the Lord would do? Not acting out of compulsion but out of love for the Savior— and out of a desire to be like Him?

Tara

The sluggard craves and gets nothing,
but the desires of the diligent are fully satisfied.

Proverbs 13:4

What do you see when you picture a rottweiler? Besides visualizing a powerfully built, brown-and-black dog, don't you see a fiercely protective, vigilant animal?

Many people have rottweilers as guard dogs or watchdogs. Tara, an eighty-five-pound rottweiler, is brown and black and does look imposing at first glance. But a watchdog she is not. Vigilance is not in her vocabulary.

Tara is not destructive in any way. She never gets into the garbage or pulls food off the table. Tara wouldn't think of chewing on the sofa or a slipper. It's neither in her nature nor on her schedule.

That's because Tara is a couch potato.

Tara's big, round bed sits in the middle of the living room. That's where you can find Tara almost twenty-four hours a day. And Tara does one thing from her private perch—when she's not sleeping. Tara watches television.

Sports, movies, the news, commercials—Tara's undivided attention focuses on the boob tube. When Morgan, Tara's owner, puts his feet up to watch some television, Tara is on her round couch relaxing as well. If Morgan gets up to work on some project for a while, Tara doesn't move from her personal couch. Television transfixes her. Nothing pulls Tara away from her spot in front of the TV.

In Proverbs, Solomon has nothing good to say about the lazy person. Under the guidance of the Holy Spirit, he admonishes the slothful person to consider one of God's smallest creatures, the ant, to get wisdom (Proverbs 6:6). We're told that the "sluggard does not plow in season" yet foolishly expects a harvest (20:4). The loafer wrongly thinks he is wise, and he frustrates those who have the misfortune to have him in their employ (26:16; 10:26).

The Lord Jesus warned us not to be lazy or lethargic when it comes to spiritual matters either. No mercy was extended to, nor excuses accepted from, the wicked, lazy servant in Matthew 25:14–30. Christ makes it clear that doing nothing with what He gives us is not just laziness but wickedness, too.

We may not have the stamina of youth to help someone. Maybe we're unable to walk a friend's dog while she recovers from surgery. Perhaps we have neither the resources to fix a meal nor the time to visit someone confined to a bed. But we can pray for each other to effect healing, and we can

> **We are to be people of proper action when possible and proper attitude perpetually.**

"be sympathetic, love as brothers, be compassionate and humble" in all our contacts (1 Peter 3:8). "We do not belong to the night or to the darkness" (1 Thessalonians 5:5). We are to be people of proper action when possible and proper attitude perpetually.

Don't be like Tara. Get up from the couch of comfort or the lounge of laziness. For the "night is coming, when no one can work" (John 9:4).

Rusty Buttons

Then Peter got down out of the boat,
walked on the water and came toward Jesus.

MATTHEW 14:29

Rusty Buttons, a blended breed of this and that, has a unique place in a family of four girls. Being the only other male in the family besides Dad, Rusty has had to adapt to the girls' interests through the years. He used to have to allow himself to be dressed up for their homespun plays. Most recently, Rusty Buttons has learned to enjoy water sports.

Rusty loves boating, the water, and the challenge of riding a surfboard behind the boat. Rusty goes after the waves alongside the boat with reckless abandon. He barks wildly as he attacks the sparkling crest of each wave that rolls or splashes by him. Once, his zeal netted him a visit to the vet because of a bad case of laryngitis. "Tell me one more time how your dog developed laryngitis?"

Rusty's preference is to one-up Kris and her sisters whenever the family is at the lake. Rusty does more than catch the waves in his teeth. He does it while he rides the surfboard—all by himself—behind their cruising speedboat. All the girls surf and ski, but only Rusty expertly surfs while maintaining his ongoing battle with chomping the foam off the top of the waves alongside him. He is not intimidated by the waves, wind, and water surrounding him. Rusty Buttons has the time of his life riding around the lake on the surfboard, looking like he was born to do it. He is fearless and happy. His merry bark reverberates around the lake as he exults in one of his favorite pastimes.

Jesus' friend Peter may have had an exhilarating experience in mind when he first stepped down from the boat onto the lake to walk on the waves to the Master. Once Peter saw the wind, however, his exhilaration turned to raw fear. Peter was not just afraid; he was terrified. In classical Greek, this word also meant to cause to run away. For Peter, there was nowhere to run. He was out of whatever protection the boat afforded him. He was in the middle of a howling wind and a cauldron of ravaging, engulfing waves. There was no happy sound emanating from Peter as he began to sink. He cried out, "Lord, save me!" (Matthew 14:30).

Have you gotten yourself in some predicament lately because of a rash decision? You may have had the Lord in view initially, but somehow you lost your focus. You went from walking boldly to sinking defenselessly. How reassuring to know that the Lord doesn't let us sink out of sight when we've gotten in over our heads. As He did with Peter, He is ready to reach out His hand and lift us up.

> How reassuring to know that the Lord doesn't let us sink out of sight when we've gotten in over our heads.

Then, like those who did not venture out of the boat, we can fall before the One who commands wind, waves, and sea, and declare, "Truly you are the Son of God" (Matthew 14:33).

Sophia

In his heart a man plans his course,
but the LORD determines his steps.
PROVERBS 16:9

They planned to erect a fence to keep their dog in the yard. Chuck and Judy planned to give their dog, Sophia, ample space to run in the confines of safety, but being practical people, they didn't want to spend a lot of money, and the chain-link fence was costly. They decided it would be best for Sophia, so they put their money concerns aside. They purchased the fence and signed the check.

Pleased with the end result once the installers finished, Judy let her beloved mongrel out. Free, without the restraint of her chain, Sophia was able to romp around the entire perimeter of the yard to her heart's content. No more limits of the leash on the clothesline. Judy smiled as Sophia scampered off the porch to sniff and snoop her way around the yard. Smiling to herself, Judy went back to her housework.

A few minutes later, Judy heard a scratching at the front door. She opened the door. There sat Sophia, tail wagging.

Uh-oh. It can't be. All that expense!

Judy let Sophia back in the house. Then she took her to the back door again and let her out. She stood back to watch.

Sophia went to the far side of the yard, galloped across

the yard's expanse at full throttle, and vaulted the fence easily. Less than a minute later, Judy heard the same scratching at the front door. She sighed. *The best-laid plans...*

Anticipating a day at the beach, preparing for a wedding, earmarking funds for the kids' education, strategizing for retirement—all of us make plans throughout our lives. Big plans and small order our days. Solomon said, "To man belong the plans of the heart" (Proverbs 16:1). Another wise person once said, "Plan like you're going to live forever; live like you're going to die tomorrow." Some of our plans bring great fruit; some are miserable failures like Chuck and Judy's chain-link fence. For some of us, our plans, like Job's, are painfully ravaged by circumstances over which we have no control. "My days have passed, my plans are shattered, and so are the desires of my heart" (Job 17:11). Job's plans dis-integrated in less time than it took to tell about them. Sometimes even well-intentioned plans are frustrated.

> **Develop your plans with the One who orders all your days.**

Our plans, from God's perspective, are all wound up in our intent. Do we plan with Him in mind, or do we carry on with God as nothing more than an afterthought?

"God is not only everywhere," a friend of mine is fond of saying, "but He is every*when*." Develop your plans with the One who orders all your days. Center your mind on the Lord, reflect on Job's words, yet still pray with hope as David does in Psalm 20:4: "May he give you the desire of your heart and make all your plans succeed."

Bonnie

But Jesus told him,
"Follow me,
and let the dead bury their own dead."
MATTHEW 8:22

No matter where Michele goes, Bonnie, a black-and-white spaniel-papillon mix, is right behind her. When Michele is home, Bonnie seldom lets her out of sight. When Michele is in the car, Bonnie rides along on her lap, her head out the window. If Michele rides her bike, Bonnie is in the canvas bag that hangs from the handlebars. All that can be seen of Bonnie is her head peeking over the top.

Michele generally takes Bonnie with her wherever she goes. If an acquaintance of Michele's welcomes Bonnie in, the little dog explores the residence thoroughly. That completed, she waits patiently by the door, watching Michele's every move to make sure Michele doesn't leave her behind. She follows her closely, carefully, and persistently.

When Michele leaves the house without her, Bonnie howls mournfully in protest. Bonnie is earnest in her intent to follow her mistress wherever and whenever she goes.

When the Lord Jesus Christ calls men and women to follow Him, He is forthright about the path ahead. "As they were walking along the road, a man said to him, 'I will follow you wherever you go.' Jesus replied, 'Foxes have holes and birds of the air have nests, but the Son of Man has no place to lay his head'" (Luke 9:57–58). Christ makes no apology—He is Lord and Master—for His demand on our lives. Although Jesus' responses—to this man and others who said they wanted to follow Him—seem harsh to us, the Lord is adamant about unreserved pursuit of Him. To be otherwise, He says, shows that we are not "fit for service in the kingdom of God" (9:62).

> When the Lord Jesus Christ calls men and women to follow Him, He is forthright about the path ahead.

To follow the Lord Jesus Christ with anything less than attentive intensity is to invite disaster. Simon Peter's ardent dedication to the Lord began to unravel when Peter allowed distance to come between him and his Master. In three of the four Gospels, we're told Peter followed Christ at a distance (Matthew 26:58; Mark 14:54; Luke 22:54). With distance between him and his leader, Peter lied and denied that he knew the Lord Jesus, finally swearing to it. This is the same Peter who once had said, "Even if I have to die with you, I will never disown you" (Mark 14:31).

With characteristic grace and love, Jesus later reinstated Peter. Even then, the issue of following Jesus came up. "Lord, what about him?" Peter asked, alluding to the apostle John. The Lord's firm response was unwavering. "If I want him to remain alive until I return, what is that to you? You must follow me" (John 21:15–22).

Peter took the Lord's words to heart. Before he died a martyr's death, he wrote to his fellow Christ followers, "To this you were called, because Christ suffered for you, leaving you an example, that you should follow in his steps" (1 Peter 2:21).

As Bonnie follows Michele, the Lord expects us to dog His every step.

Sin and Its Cleansing

Sin is like dog poo;
when you get some on your shoe,
a little is as bad as a lot.

CHUCK MILLER

Lucy

*Here is a trustworthy saying
that deserves full acceptance:
Christ Jesus came into the world to save sinners.*
1 TIMOTHY 1:15

She's as cute a puppy as you would ever want to see. Lucy, a black Labrador, is all soft fur and big, brown eyes—and she's growing like a weed. But looks aren't everything, as Ed and Kristin are learning. Lucy has a destructive bent.

Lucy is showered daily with love and attention from the entire family. They purchased her with hard-earned cash and made sure she received all her shots. They provide her with water, food, and shelter. She's special to the family; she's their only pet. The kids coddle and cuddle her. Lucy is loved and cared for. It's been no small sacrifice for Kristin and company to welcome Lucy into their home.

So why does Lucy chew on couch pillows when she has toys to chew on?

Why does Lucy eat a pair of shoes when she has food for consumption?

Why does Lucy eat a second pair of shoes after being punished for eating the first pair?

When Lucy is provided with everything she wants, as

well as the kindness, love, and shelter she needs, why does Lucy continue her wreckage? She is a puppy, but even puppies must learn. Lucy knows when she does wrong—repentance is written all over her face. It's obvious by the hanging of her head. She receives her deserved punishment. She receives her correction and instruction. Lucy behaves. . .for a day. . .or an hour.

Then Lucy returns to her destructive mode and receives her deserved punishment again.

Does this pattern sound familiar, even if you don't have a puppy?

God tells us we, too, have a bent toward destruction. He calls it sin. Speaking of all people, God says, "Every inclination of his heart is evil from childhood" (Genesis 8:21). "There is no one who does good," declared David in Psalm 14:1. In the New Testament, we are reminded, "All have sinned and fall short of the glory of God" (Romans 3:23). Our sin hurts us, hurts others, and pains the heart of God Almighty. The Lord's grief can be heard in His question and command to Israel: "Why will you die. . . ? For I take no pleasure in the death of anyone, declares the Sovereign LORD. Repent and live!" (Ezekiel 18:31–32).

Repentance extends beyond hanging our heads and looking sorry. It entails a change of attitude and conduct. Repentance that changed everything is seen in the life of one of the thieves who died alongside Jesus and in the life of the apostle Paul. Judas Iscariot's "repentance" changed nothing. "Godly sorrow brings repentance that leads to salvation and leaves no regret, but worldly sorrow brings death" (2 Corinthians 7:10).

When you repent of sin before God today, don't be like Lucy, who makes a show of being sorry. Be genuine. God stands ready to forgive the person who has "a broken and contrite heart" (Psalm 51:17).

> Be genuine. God stands ready to forgive the person who has "a broken and contrite heart" (Psalm 51:17).

Kontou and Tara

The blood of Jesus Christ his Son
cleanseth us from all sin.

1 John 1:7 KJV

Kontou and Tara, two Alaskan malamutes with a propensity for getting into trouble, had done it again. They had run off to do some exploring. Now Char and Ed had the unenviable task of tracking from farm to farm to find their two rascals.

Being the male, Kontou is bigger than Tara. He's usually the ringleader when it comes to making a mess or getting into a fix. One Christmas, Char stepped out of the kitchen momentarily while the turkey cooled a bit. The turkey had no time to cool. Kontou pulled it off the counter, awarding Tara one drumstick while he devoured the rest.

On another occasion, Kontou and Tara had hitched a ride in the back of a stranger's pickup only to end up in a town miles from their home. They almost found themselves in two new homes, separated for good. This time the search was, fortunately, much shorter than the earlier one. Char and Ed came home after being unsuccessful in locating the two runaways, but soon a man in a sports car approached.

"You the folks looking for some dogs?" he asked.

Char answered affirmatively.

"Well, they're at my place," he said. "You're gonna have to come and get 'em. I wasn't about to put 'em in my car. They're in my pigsty."

Char and Ed almost drowned Kontou and Tara in tomato juice. But the stench didn't wash out that easily. The two miscreants were bundled in blankets and hauled home. It would be some time and a lot of suds and water before their dogs didn't smell like pigs.

In Jude, some of scripture's most severe words are leveled against those who are "godless men, who change the grace of our God into a license for immorality and deny Jesus Christ our only Sovereign and Lord" (Jude 4). Ungodly leaders have been duping and misleading people for centuries. For those who fall under their influence, we are to show mercy, even while we hate "the clothing stained by corrupted flesh" (verse 23). God never minces words when it comes to the defiling effects of sin.

Like Kontou and Tara, covered with the filth and stench of the pigpen, we are stained and dirty with sin. Sin's stain and stench, both on us and in us, cannot be washed away by our actions or merit. Only Jesus' blood can cleanse us.

Once we confess our sin, God "is faithful and just and will forgive us our sins and purify us from all unrighteousness" (1 John 1:9). It is the blood of Christ that effects our cleansing (1:7). In contrast to the infiltrators mentioned in

Jude's letter, John is shown those "who have come out of the great tribulation; they have washed their robes and made them white in the blood of the Lamb" (Revelation 7:14).

When God cleanses people, the cleansing is complete.

> When God cleanses people, the cleansing is complete.

Cooper

*"Your own conduct and actions
have brought this upon you.
This is your punishment."*
JEREMIAH 4:18

It was the last straw!

Kelly's yellow Labrador retriever, Cooper, had strewn garbage all over the kitchen one time too many. When he was six months old, Cooper went from innocent puppy to renegade dog—tearing up, chewing up, and messing up the house from kitchen to bedroom. If Kelly left food on the counter, Cooper clambered up to get it. Her collection of childhood stuffed animals became Cooper's teething rings. The kitchen garbage became his afternoon snack.

Kelly tried everything she knew to get Cooper to behave. Swatting him with a rolled-up newspaper didn't work. Scolding him didn't work. The time had come for the hard-nosed approach. Kelly bought a remote-controlled shock collar.

If there's anything else that can be said about Cooper, it's that he learns quickly. He only had to wear the shock collar once. Kelly used it only once. With one well-timed punishment to fit the crime, Kelly's angel dog was back—for a few weeks.

Cooper returned to his old tricks. Kelly came home to find aluminum foil pulled out of the kitchen trash can and shredded all over the floor. Disobedience had again reared its ugly head. She sighed and got the collar out of the cupboard.

Cooper took off running! He dodged Kelly. He slithered out of her grasp. He ducked when she reached for him. Finally, he dove under the kitchen table, planting himself out of reach. His mischievous brown eyes—now all innocence and remorse—begged Kelly to let bygones be bygones.

To be on the giving end of punishment is seldom any easier than being on the receiving end. But sin necessitates punishment. From Adam and Eve's first day in the garden, God made it known that sin would be punished. To fall short of or to offend God's surpassing holiness brings deserved punishment. "I will punish the world for its evil," God declares, "the wicked for their sins" (Isaiah 13:11). For sins of sexual immorality, we're told, "The Lord will punish men for all such sins. . . For God did not call us to be impure, but to live a holy life" (1 Thessalonians 4:6–7). God punishes less obvious sins such as complacency (Zephaniah 1:12) and indifference (Matthew 25:41–46), too.

> **God is just;**
> **God is holy.**

God is just; God is holy. He is out to make us reflect His perfectly obedient Son, Jesus Christ. Kelly could no more let Cooper carry on with his bad behavior than

God can overlook ours. Christ has taken our ultimate punishment—eternal separation from the living God—by His death on the cross. God does forgive. God even forgets (Isaiah 43:25). The repentant thief on the cross was forgiven, but he died that day on the cross for his sins against the state.

Let bygones be bygones? Little oversights, unkind thoughts, or blatant acts of disobedience have consequences. They will be punished. Why? God is out to collar us that we might be "conformed to the likeness of His Son" (Romans 8:29).

Mollyanna

His divine power has given us
everything we need for life
and godliness through our knowledge of him
who called us by his own glory and goodness.

2 PETER 1:3

After thirteen years, Becky and Brett lost their black Labrador. They decided they didn't want another dog. Dealing with the death of a pet simply wasn't worth it. Not much time passed before the couple reconsidered. Perhaps they should get another dog, another black Lab.

But it could only be a calm dog—one like their last pet.

That's when they got Mollyanna, everything they had hoped for in a new dog. She's sweet natured, obedient, and not at all destructive. She doesn't chew on furniture or shoes. She doesn't jump on guests. Mollyanna is calm.

There's only one small problem.

Mollyanna has a fixation with electrical cords. She never leaves them alone when they're plugged into a wall socket. The first time Brett and Becky came home after leaving Mollyanna free in the house for a few hours, they found every lamp, small appliance, and electrical device within reach of Mollyanna's teeth unplugged. There was no damage, no teeth marks on the electrical cords, nothing out of place. But the house was dark. The lights had been cut off from their power source.

"At just the right time, when we were still powerless, Christ died for the ungodly" (Romans 5:6). Even the most well-meaning, moral, "good" people among us cannot escape the simple fact that we are sinners. As sinners, we are powerless to meet the demands of a holy God. Even as Christ followers, we struggle with sin.

In his letter to the Christians at Rome, Paul said it this way: "I do not understand what I do.... For what I do is not the good I want to do; no, the evil I do not want to do—this I keep on doing" (Romans 7:15, 19). The Bible makes it clear that we cannot do good or be godly in

> Goodness can only flow in and through us when we're connected to the sole power source of goodness: the Lord Jesus Christ.

our own power. It's simply not in us—before we become Christians or afterward. The apostle Paul concluded, "What a wretched man I am!" (7:24).

Goodness can only flow in and through us when we're connected to the sole power source of goodness: the Lord Jesus Christ. Jesus said, "Apart from me you can do nothing" (John 15:5). We may hear or read about the "basic goodness" of people, but that's a contradiction. In Genesis, God's assessment of men (and women) is that "every inclination of the thoughts of his heart was only evil all the time" (Genesis 6:5). Every inclination. . .only evil. . .all the time. So much for our innate goodness. God says we are powerless to be good.

Yet we can say with Paul, "Thanks be to God—through Jesus Christ our Lord!" (Romans 7:25). By being connected to the source of all goodness, we are empowered to be full of goodness like the Christians to whom Paul wrote the book of Romans.

Not at all like the powerless household lamps of calm (but ornery) Mollyanna.

Lady Anne

*Now Israel loved Joseph
more than all his children. . .
and he made him a coat of many colours.*
GENESIS 37:3 KJV

Lady Anne is the progeny of black and yellow Labrador retrievers. Always ready to play, Lady Anne meets her owner at the door when Gina comes home after working the midnight shift. Lady has a ball in her mouth, ready to romp. Midnight shift has no meaning for her.

Recently Gina took Lady Anne along to pick up Gina's daughter at school. The school, with its large grassy area, provided the perfect space for Lady Anne to run. Ten minutes hadn't passed before Gina looked up to see Lady rolling in the grass.

Oh no!

Gina was sure Lady Anne was rolling in some odoriferous pile of something or other. As dog owner hastened to dog, however, no odor assaulted Gina's nose. Gina's initial relief was brief. An unexpected sight assailed her eyes. Her beautiful golden-and-black Labrador had an orange-and-green rump and a bright-blue neck. Evidently an art class had slopped an assortment of paints on the ground. That was what Lady Anne had discovered and was so gleefully rolling in. Her fur was matted with an array of hues.

Lady Anne had a new coat of many colors!

When left to our own devices, whether we are people or pets, we don't usually choose to do the right thing, or even the smart thing. We never have to teach our pets to do the bad thing; it comes naturally to them. We don't have to teach children how to do wrong. Early on, every toy is "mine!" Selfishness, greed, and doing things our way come quite easily for all of us who share this space we call earth.

"Man is born to trouble as surely as sparks fly upward," we're told in Job 5:7. David, who was commended by God as a man after His own heart, knew that he was sinful at birth (Psalm 51:5). "Moses, whom the LORD knew face to face," was not permitted to enter the Promised Land because of his sin (Deuteronomy 32:50–52; 34:10).

> Yet before the Lord started time, He knew He would have to make provision for our sin.

Sin has infected us since our common parents, Adam and Eve, walked in the garden. Yet before the Lord started time, He knew He would have to make provision for our sin. The Lord Jesus Christ is "the Lamb that was slain from the creation of the world" (Revelation 13:8). He purifies us from all iniquity and unrighteousness.

Gina had her work cut out for her. She gave Lady Anne a good scrubbing to restore her to her original, God-given coat. Often the Lord has to clean us up after we've been guilty of rolling in the world's dirt. Someday our cleansing will be complete. We will stand before the throne, in front of the Lamb, wearing white robes (Revelation 7:9).

Hallelujah!

Kenmore

*"I will repay you for the years
the locusts have eaten. . .
and you will praise the name
of the LORD your God,
who has worked wonders for you."*

JOEL 2:25–26

Kenmore (not his real name) got himself into some serious trouble. The little white Pekingese dog got behind Charlene's washing machine and was caught. To make matters worse, the machine had been running, and so the poor little guy was stuck fast and possibly injured. Charlene, unsure of what to do by herself, called those rescuers of the big and small, the well and ill: her local fire department.

With nervous trepidation, Charlene watched while the firefighters meticulously took apart the back of her washer to free Kenmore. To her profound relief, they were able to extract her pet alive from the gears. Kenmore was understandably shaken, and his poor tail was shaved hairless to the skin, but he was well. He was saved!

Charlene thanked her dog's heroes profusely as she held her quivering little dog to her chest. With their customary humility, the firefighters waved off her gratitude and started for the door. Charlene looked at her washer—now disassembled in a hundred or so pieces.

"What. . .what about my washing machine being all torn apart?" she asked weakly.

The exiting firefighters glanced back at the nuts and bolts all over the floor. Again, with their customary humility (and possibly just the smallest facetious intent), the exiting firefighters shrugged their shoulders in apology. The last one gave her their parting farewell: "We don't do washers."

People, too, get entrapped. We may inadvertently step into the middle of a cold war between family members or friends, and then, like it or not, find ourselves forced to choose sides. A child tells a lie, gets caught in it, and tries to backpedal with another falsehood. And how often we all get caught in the Blame Game. We're like Adam: "The woman you put here with me"—or Eve: "The serpent deceived me" (Genesis 3:12–13).

> **How reassuring the words of scripture that one day the Lord will make everything new!**

Whether we sin intentionally or in ignorance, our mistakes, errors in judgment, and sins carry consequences, sometimes for life's duration. "You may be sure that your sin will find you out," Moses warns us (Numbers 32:23).

How reassuring the words of scripture that one day the Lord will make everything new! How blessed to know the promises of God that declare such wonderful truths as these:

"I will forgive their wickedness and will remember their sins no more" (Jeremiah 31:34).

Jesus Christ "gave himself for us to redeem us from all wickedness" (Titus 2:14).

"In repentance and rest is your salvation" (Isaiah 30:15).

The Lord Jesus Christ has made a way for us to one day be free from sin and all its effects—and from our foolish or unintentional mistakes and all those consequences.

Unlike the well-intentioned firefighters (who admittedly had more serious duties to attend to), the Lord Jesus won't leave any pieces strewn about. Wholeness, completeness, and fulfillment await those "who hold to the testimony of Jesus" (Revelation 19:10).

The Fruit of the Spirit

*I rest my hand on my collie's
trusting head and I see love, joy,
peace, patience, kindness, goodness,
faithfulness, gentleness, and self-control.*

CHUCK MILLER

Lady

But the fruit of the Spirit is love.

GALATIANS 5:22

Her name is not Lady Love, but it could be. Lady, a buff-colored cocker spaniel, has loved her owner, Sue, since she was small enough to be held in one of Sue's hands. Lady demonstrates her love in simple ways. Like so many of her kind, she knows just what is needed and when.

When tears fall, Lady dries them in her own loving way. If Sue is weeping, Lady jumps up on her owner's lap. She very gently places one paw on one of Sue's shoulders and one on the other. She ever so gently licks the tears from Sue's face. Then she nestles her head comfortingly under Sue's chin.

Sue has one rule about sleeping: no dogs in the bed. Being a very light sleeper, anything and everything wakes her up. It's a puzzle, therefore, when she wakes up in the morning to find Lady burrowed under the covers. Her head is on the pillow, lovingly snuggled between Sue and her husband. Whenever Sue returns home from anywhere, Lady is unfailingly at the window, her face a picture of expectant love.

Sue loves Lady. And Lady most certainly loves Sue. God is love.

More songs have been written, more stories told, more poetry penned, and more thoughts pondered on those three words than any other three in any tongue ever uttered by men or angels. How can we presume to compare any love we have known here on earth to that of the Creator who is love itself? Words and illustrations fail, though the birth, life, death, and resurrection of Jesus Christ show that God is love most fully.

| God is love. |

Grace was a missionary to India for decades. She and her husband saw precious little fruit from their ministry while living on earth, but they remained true to God's calling.

Two things stood out about Grace. First, she would not drink anything with caffeine in it. Grace was not a nurse, but she knew, years before decaf-anything was available, that caffeine is a powerful medicinal stimulant. She drank Postum, a hot, caffeine-free beverage. Second, Grace did not like to sing songs such as "Oh, How I Love Jesus." Grace, who had dedicated her life unreservedly to the Lord, said it this way: "How can we sing about our love for God? Our love is so paltry compared to His love for us!"

Grace was very uncomfortable singing about loving God. But when it was time to sing of God's love for us, Grace was ready to be choir, choir director, and congregation. That, she could sing about exuberantly!

"This is love: not that we loved God, but that he loved us and sent his Son as an atoning sacrifice for our sins" (1 John 4:10).

God keeps a record of our tears. He quiets us with His love and rejoices over us with singing (Psalm 56:8; Zephaniah 3:17).

Inky

But the fruit of the Spirit is. . .joy.

GALATIANS 5:22

Up in the air she leaps! Inky, a black-and-white Australian shepherd, loves to catch her green tennis ball when it flies through the air. She becomes airborne, too, and snatches her ball out of midair with practiced grace. Golden brown eyes sparkling and silky fur waving, she races back joyfully to Daryl for another toss. She practically grins as she eagerly awaits another throw of the ball.

Inky is joyful about everything in life. She barks very little, but she merrily tears about in reckless abandon whenever she's outside. First thing in the morning, she can be seen at a dead run, heading out to the field behind the pond. When Daryl, a truck driver by occupation, is ready to leave, Inky is quick to leap into the seat beside him. Inky is a seasoned traveler. She is as joyous about riding alongside Daryl in his eighteen-wheeler as she is about jumping up to catch her tennis ball or beating her companion shepherd in their morning run. Joy is one word that describes Inky from the tip of her shiny nose to the end of her stubby tail.

Joy is crucial to our daily existence. Joyfulness exceeds happiness in that happiness is often little more than freedom from sadness or sorrow. Joy is deeper, more resilient. We can have joy when we have little or no cause to be happy. Think of the apostle Paul, whose letter to the church in Philippi rings with joy. Joy and its derivative words occur throughout this epistle, written by Paul the prisoner. "I always pray with joy because of your partnership in the gospel," he said (Philippians 1:4–5). Even though he compared himself to being poured out like a drink offering, he rejoiced and remained glad. Paul wasn't about to allow his stay in prison to rob him of his joy. He refused to let his circumstances define his attitude.

Our joy, like Paul's, must come from deep within—and from a basis of reality—to be of genuine, sustaining worth. We need joy that sustains us when people, circumstances, or health fail us. Surely, at some point, all these will fail us. When these disappointments, discouragements, or illnesses muscle their way into our lives, we need a joy that remains unshaken and unshakable.

We need the kind of joy that sustained the Lord Jesus Christ when His foes appeared to gain the upper hand and His dearest friends deserted Him. Did He still possess joy? Was it a joy steeped in reality that kept Him going in His darkest hour? The Word says yes: Jesus, "who for the joy set before him endured the cross" (Hebrews 12:2).

> By fixing our eyes on Jesus, the author and perfecter of our faith, we won't grow weary or lose heart.

By fixing our eyes on Jesus, the author and perfecter of our faith, we won't grow weary or lose heart. It's how we nurture joy in a joyless world.

Like Inky, we nurture joy by sitting in the truck cab, contentedly looking toward home.

Tanner and Pepper

But the fruit of the Spirit is. . .peace.
GALATIANS 5:22

Without knowing all the facts, people might think Tanner and Pepper are overly coddled. They are fed the best food available and regularly bathed, groomed, and taken to the vet. They have the distinction of having their own room—not a doghouse, not a corner, but their own room. They don't share it with any human. It's theirs exclusively. Tanner and Pepper are privileged, pampered pets. Tanner is so privileged and pampered that he's been put on a diet. (He gained thirty pounds in less than a year. Tanner cannot resist any treat—whether he should have it or not.)

Some may think Tanner and Pepper are spoiled. Some might protest that mere dogs should not be treated so lavishly. Some might say someone has gone overboard in extravagant provision for these two golden retrievers. And some might be right. Until they learn what Tanner and Pepper do for a living.

Tanner and Pepper are hospice dogs. They reside in a lovely, end-of-life sanctuary where they go to a human's room and do what they can to bring peace and quietude. Sometimes one of them will lie at the foot of a patient's bed. Tanner will allow a sufferer to stroke his head over and over again. Pepper will snuggle his wet nose under a still hand and remain there like a sentinel of peace. Both dogs are always ready, day or night, to administer the calming peace that their presence brings to so many people in their final days.

> **When peace washes over us, it is a heavenly balm.**

When peace washes over us, it is a heavenly balm. "In this world you will have trouble" the Lord said, "[but] in me you may have peace" (John 16:33). The "peace of God, which transcends all understanding" (Philippians 4:7), is an unmatched gift.

Laurie lost her father suddenly. He was taken to the hospital emergency center one afternoon. Initially her father was alert and talking. Then he was transferred to intensive care, deteriorating rapidly. Laurie and her family were overwhelmed with the speed at which events were happening. In a nightmarish daze, Laurie called a friend, a nurse in another unit at that hospital.

"I think," Laurie told her friend brokenly, "I think my dad is dying!"

Susie was at the side of Laurie and her family immediately. Susie prayed, and peace came. Peace so overwhelming it was palpable. Laurie's dad was not miraculously healed. He stood in eternal, robust health beside his Lord that night. But for Laurie and her family, the peace was still there, sustaining them through their loss. "A heart at peace gives life to the body" (Proverbs 14:30).

If, like Susie, you are blessed with the gift of peace, give it to someone today. If you need it, be ready to receive it. It may come in the words of a friend's prayer or in the touch of a wet nose under your hand.

Buff

But the fruit of the Spirit is. . .patience.
GALATIANS 5:22

Buff is a dog of mixed breed. He's a long-haired, buff-colored mongrel of indeterminate origin. Buff's owners, Jim and Casey, know that Buff, despite his unknown heritage, is a dog of true breeding. These two brothers don't mind that Buff doesn't have an impressive lineage. Buff's patience is pedigree enough for them.

In storm, sunshine, or snow, Jim and Casey know Buff will be waiting for them at the bus stop when they come home from school. Whether the weather is favorable or not, Buff sits patiently awaiting his two young charges. If the school bus is running a little late or a little early, Buff is always there, Monday through Friday. He doesn't miss a school day, and he never misses being the first one to greet Jim and Casey after their day at school. Jim and Casey never taught Buff how to tell time. They never taught him patience. They never even taught him to come to the bus stop. Buff just does it. And when Jim and Casey's school bus comes around the corner, Buff is one tail-wagging, happy mongrel.

Denise is patiently plugging away at getting her college

degree. She is a single mother with four growing children of grade-school age. Denise takes good care of her kids, carefully monitors their progress in school, and diligently attends all parent-teacher conferences for each child. She's always there to cheer her children on during their recreational activities. Denise holds down a full-time paying job in addition to the one she does at home (for free). But Denise aspires to do more for herself and her family. Every year, a few hours this semester, a couple hours the next semester, Denise patiently works to complete her college education. She may not finish before the last of her children has graduated from high school, but she is determined to persevere, to painstakingly, patiently finish what she started.

> Our entire history is a study of the astounding patience of God.

In the meantime, however, she is not about to miss the importance of patiently cherishing the everyday rewards of motherhood along the way.

In almost every New Testament use of "patience," when applied to the Lord God, the word is used in the context of God's patience with those who are indifferent to or who rebuff His love. "Bear in mind that our Lord's patience means salvation," Peter said (2 Peter 3:15). While Noah built his lifesaving ark, God waited patiently for repentance from people, which never came. God is patient—lovingly patient—not wanting anyone to perish. Our entire history is a study of the astounding patience of God.

Our instruction from God is to "be patient, bearing with one another in love" (Ephesians 4:2). We are to clothe ourselves with patience (Colossians 3:12). Today when your patience is sorely tested, reflect on God's magnanimous patience. Remember the patience of a single mom who won't quit.

Picture Buff, waiting patiently for that big yellow bus.

Pudge

But the fruit of the Spirit is. . .kindness.
GALATIANS 5:22

Pudge never read anywhere that dogs aren't supposed to like cats. He doesn't know that as a dog he should not be kind to any felines. A gentle creature by nature, Pudge watched Fudge with her new litter of kittens. He watched, and he learned.

Whenever Fudge leaves her brood for short periods, Pudge steps in and takes over. If Fudge leaves the basket of kittens to get food, Pudge immediately assumes her nurturing stance. He climbs into the basket, allowing the kittens to snuggle in around him. It doesn't matter to Pudge that he has no nourishment for the litter. Neither do they seem to mind. They huddle eagerly next to Pudge, glad for the warmth of his presence and his unassuming kindness to them.

Now that the kittens are older and no longer interested in another warm body when Fudge has gone her own way, Pudge still treats them kindly. He defers to their rambunctious play and insatiable curiosity. He never teases or torments any of these mewing fur balls. Pudge is kindness itself when it comes to these little ones he's helped nurture since they were "pups."

In the King James Version of the Bible, kindness is rendered "gentleness." Aside from kindness itself, the multiple meanings of this word include qualities such as benignity or harmlessness and usefulness. Biblical kindness is not related to deeds but rather describes a person's disposition.

Kindness, by its very nature, may permeate another person or the atmosphere in a room of people by its very unobtrusiveness. It steals over us like a fluid fog moving across a field of winter wheat. Its refreshing balm is hard to describe outside of words such as "gentleness," "peace," and "cleansing." There are few who can resist the gentle grace of kindness. It is the most beneficent fruit of the Spirit.

> Kindness.
> The irresistible
> gentle giant.

Pastor Jim emanates kindness. A tall man with a deeply resonant voice, his every mannerism bespeaks the kindness that so permeates his disposition. When he refers to his congregation as "his people," it is a term of endearment and not an occasion to boast about or bemoan those to whom he ministers. Jim is the quintessential gentle giant.

Emily, a three-year-old dying of an inoperable brain tumor, would not eat. No amount of coercion or enticement from her parents, grandparents, or caregivers could persuade her otherwise. Frustrated with this additional ordeal in the long nightmare that had come to mark Emily's last days, her mom and dad finally gave up trying to compel their daughter to eat.

Pastor Jim walked into Emily's hospital room. He sat down beside this little girl who was one of the youngest of his people. He picked up Emily's spoon and scooped some food onto it.

"Would you eat some for me, Emily?" Jim asked.

Emily smiled. Emily ate.

Kindness. The irresistible gentle giant.

Hershey and Mattie

But the fruit of the Spirit is. . .goodness.
GALATIANS 5:22

Hershey is a well-behaved, good dog. He never snaps at or bites people or other animals. He extends his paw for a handshake when commanded and barks for a biscuit if and when he wants one. He is a chocolate Lab who is a credit to his kind. When his owner gives Hershey a pat on the head and says, "Good dog," he means it. Hershey is a good dog.

Mattie is not a good dog. She is rambunctious, ornery, and always ready to chomp on the wrong thing. Hershey doesn't lose patience with Mattie when she bites him. He never retaliates. He doesn't growl. That's because Hershey is a good dog. Fortunately, Hershey is teaching Mattie and not the other way around.

By example, Hershey is teaching Mattie how to shake hands, how to bark for a treat, and how to play tug-of-war with a rope. Their owner doesn't have to command Mattie to shake. Mattie has learned to put her paw up when she arrives at the biscuit corner, and she barks without the customary "Speak!" command. She learned from watching Hershey. And Hershey is teaching Mattie to use her teeth on their play toy—not on him or others.

By daily example, Hershey is teaching Mattie how to be a good dog.

Goodness manifests itself in Betty's life every day. Betty is into her seventies and is always actively doing good. Micah the prophet said God "has showed you. . .what is good. [It is] to act justly and to love mercy and to walk humbly with your God" (Micah 6:8). Betty's life of service to others demonstrates goodness. If she isn't working with children or helping out at an extended-care facility, she's baking something for someone or chauffeuring friends who are unable to drive. Nieces, from thirty to more than sixty years old, call their aunt from three states away because she has always been good to them. A golfer herself, she takes her great-grandson golfing. The "fruit of the light consists in all goodness" (Ephesians 5:9) in Betty. Her God-given goodness attracts people of all ages to her—and draws them closer to the Source of all goodness.

> When we radiate goodness, others are drawn to Him who is the sum total of all goodness.

When Moses asked God to show him His glory, the Lord said, "I will cause all my goodness to pass in front of you" (Exodus 33:19). Moses' face was radiant from the experience. When we radiate goodness, others are drawn to Him who is the sum total of all goodness. The Lord Jesus said, "Let your light shine before men, that they may see your good deeds and praise your Father in heaven"

(Matthew 5:16). As with other fruit of the Spirit, goodness may be an innate quality, but it shows itself in actions:

An older dog playing with a younger one.

A septuagenarian taking a teenager golfing.

The Lord who "causes his sun to rise on the evil and the good, and sends rain on the righteous and the unrighteous" (Matthew 5:45).

Sadie

But the fruit of the Spirit is. . .faithfulness.
GALATIANS 5:22

Sadie is as faithful as a pet can be. Whenever Chuck comes home from work, his chocolate cocker spaniel beats a path to the door to greet him. She's not about to be outdone or outrun by anyone else. Chuck and his wife, Carol, are the two most important people in Sadie's life. She is their faithful, trustworthy dog.

Sadie is faithful in the big and little things. She brings her own food and water dishes to Chuck or Carol when they need to be filled. There's never a worry about Sadie getting into trouble at night. Sadie sleeps in the closet every night—by her own unexplainable choice. There aren't a whole lot of surprises in life with Sadie. She's trustworthy, dependable, faithful to a fault. She never takes off, leaving her owners to search for her. Sadie is a faithful homebody. She never snaps at or bites little ones. She can be trusted with the grandkids. She's proven it time and again.

In Titus 2:9–10 the Greek word for "faithfulness" (*pistis*) gives us a vivid word picture of faithfulness in action. "Teach slaves to be subject to their masters in everything, to try to please them, not to talk back to them, and not to steal from them, but to show that they can be fully trusted." In the King James Version, the final phrase reads, "shewing all good fidelity." That was quite an order for a slave, one who by definition was deemed not a person but a living tool—one who had no rights whatsoever. Still, that's how Christian slaves are instructed to behave.

Faithfulness is such a beautiful character quality, yet how rare it is today. Men and women are unfaithful to their spouses. Honorable employers cannot always trust their employees to conduct business as reputably as they do; good employees cannot always trust a shrewd employer to deal honestly with them. The media cannot be trusted to report the news with impartiality. The courts do not always protect the victim and punish the victimizer. Too often faithfulness and trustworthiness are practiced only when it's convenient or a means to another end—not because it's right. Not because it's Christlike.

> Faithfulness is such a beautiful character quality, yet how rare it is today.

What an encouragement to know Someone you can depend on no matter what. The Lord Jesus had nothing but the highest praise for those who are faithful in the minutiae. They can be trusted with much. Even if faithfulness is a fruit we do not think we possess in abundance, the Lord still commands us to "be faithful, even to the point of death" (Revelation 2:10). We are to be faithful—people of fidelity.

Sadie is faithful in big and small ways. We can be, too. We only need to ask God, "who gives generously to all without finding fault" (James 1:5), for He is the "faithful God who does no wrong" (Deuteronomy 32:4).

Teddy

But the fruit of the Spirit is. . .gentleness.
GALATIANS 5:22–23

From the time he was a puppy, Teddy the basset hound has exuded gentleness. If Katy, Teddy's owner, is feeling blue, Teddy is right there with his head on her lap. If she is upset, Teddy senses it and lies beside her quietly. Teddy's one consistent character quality is gentleness. He showers his gentleness particularly upon Rachel.

Rachel came wandering into the yard from the adjacent field when she was a scrawny, woebegone kitten. At first she was afraid of everything and everyone, especially Teddy. But hunger or curiosity, or both, drove Rachel closer and closer each day, first to nibble at the food that was invitingly put out for her, then to follow quietly behind Katy and Teddy when they went for their walks. Teddy has never been one to fight a turf war with another creature. When Rachel began following him during his walks with Katy, he gently allowed the scraggly, uninvited guest to tag along right behind them.

Once Rachel became an official member of the family, Teddy extended his gentleness to her as he does to everyone. Now Rachel sidles up to Teddy every chance she gets. If she's cold, she curls up under his chin. If she wants the double warmth of sunlight and Teddy, she makes herself at home on Teddy's back under the warm autumn sun. Teddy doesn't begrudge Rachel her place on his back or under his nose. He is Rachel's gentle companion.

Gentleness. In the King James Version translation of Galatians 5:23, the word is translated "meekness." *Meekness* is a word pregnant with meaning in New Testament Greek. Here it means mildness or forbearance. It has less to do with an outward manifestation than it does "an inward grace of the soul, calmness toward God in particular" (from Zodhiates, *The Complete Word Study Dictionary*).

Calmness toward God...inward grace of the soul. Aren't we all drawn to people who, like Teddy the basset hound, exude gentleness? People with whom we can bare our souls or share our deepest secrets? People who reassure us of God's control and God's purpose and God's tender love by their very lives? Perhaps you are a person with this gift, or perhaps you thought you had this gift and feel you've somehow lost it along the way.

> Calmness toward God. . .inward grace of the soul.

The definition of gentleness—meekness—in *The Complete Word Study Dictionary* goes on to say that it is the "acceptance of God's dealings with us considering them as good in that they enhance the closeness of our relationship with Him." Intriguing, isn't it, that the fruit of the Spirit has as much to do with our vertical relationship—the Lord—as it does with our horizontal relationships—people.

You may think of Teddy and Rachel when gentleness shows itself today. But think, too, of the Lord who said, "Take my yoke upon you and learn from me, for I am gentle [meek] and humble in heart, and you will find rest for your souls" (Matthew 11:29).

Chilo

But the fruit of the Spirit is. . .self-control.

GALATIANS 5:22–23

*B*eing half Weimaraner and half German shorthaired pointer, Chilo is the consummate hunting dog. Faster on her feet than a jackrabbit, quick to retrieve fowl and small game, able to snatch a low-flying bird out of the air like a Frisbee, Chilo is Alan's finest hunting dog. Chilo loves to hunt, and she loves her master. From her master, she has learned marvelous self-control.

Alan's wife doesn't need to worry about Chilo snatching up a dropped piece of food on the kitchen floor. Chilo won't go near it—even if it's a favorite treat—unless she's permitted. Alan can balance a piece of meat on Chilo's nose, and she'll leave it there until he says, "Okay!" If Alan then says, "Spit it out," Chilo does just that. Chilo is not given to gluttony; Chilo is self-controlled.

Chilo is dangerously protective of Alan. Readying for a hunt one morning, Alan was on one side of his truck, and Chilo was on the other. The local game warden approached Alan to check his hunting license. The warden was out of Alan's field of vision but not Chilo's.

Alan turned abruptly when he heard Chilo's ferocious bark.

"Stay!"

Chilo stopped immediately.

Alan's command was not a second too soon. Chilo was ready to attack the armed stranger. For his part, the game warden had reached for his gun in self-defense.

The game warden apologized to Alan for his blunder. He knew better than to approach as he had. He was especially glad (as was Alan) that Chilo's self-control was so well ingrained.

We are quick to admire people who exercise the more winsome of the fruit of the Spirit: patience, kindness, gentleness. We appreciate self-control (especially if we lack it), but it's not a gift that commands attention—possibly because its exercise is often unseen.

Rodd and Lisa's teenage daughter disappeared. Her Bible was found laying on the ground beside her friend's parked car, but both girls were missing. Terrified and praying, Rodd and Lisa began trying to retrace their daughter's steps from the previous evening. As they did so, Lisa was praying feverishly for her daughter's safety.

> Calmness toward God. . .inward grace of the soul.

Shaking with fear and rage, Rodd was asking God to help him not kill the abductor, if indeed there was one.

Thankfully, the girls were safe and there had been no foul play, just missed communication and miscommunication. Yet few would know how Rodd mentally struggled with his possession (or lack) of self-control in those harrowing hours of the unknown.

"Like a city whose walls are broken down is a man who lacks self-control" (Proverbs 25:28). "But since we belong to the day, let us be self-controlled" (1 Thessalonians 5:8).

When it comes to self-control, we need to be prepared ahead of time. The next time the game warden saw Alan and Chilo, he was all smiles and forethought. He gave Alan a friendly wave.

"Don't need to check you," he said. "I remember your dog."

Talking the Walk

Why are we so afraid—
unlike my collie—
to let everyone, and anyone,
know where we've been
and the route we took to get there?

CHUCK MILLER

Jessie

*"When someone invites you to a wedding feast,
do not take the place of honor,
for a person more distinguished
than you may have been invited."*

LUKE 14:8

Jessie, a marbled Australian shepherd, is a dog with a penchant for the unusual. Although she is a member of a family made up of a dad, a mom, two boys, and a girl, Jessie definitely knows her place as a female member of the household.

As happens so frequently when groups of people get together, when Sharon and her husband have company, the women invariably gather in one room to talk and the men in the other. Jessie sits herself down among the women and attends to the conversation as if she is following every word of it. If there is a hen session in the house, as it used to be called, there's Jessie, right in the middle, contributing little but absorbing everything—or giving the appearance that she's doing so.

Jessie's other peculiar habit has to do with photography. No matter who has the camera, what's being photographed, or if the pictures are taken inside or out, when the developed pictures come back, there's Jessie. She's front and center if she can get away with it. If not, she still manages to get her face in the picture somehow, somewhere. When the camera comes out, Jessie is ready to pose to her best advantage in every photo—invited or not.

The picture is perfectly clear: Jessie wants to be seen.

Mark is a most unusual man for our culture. There is absolutely nothing pretentious about him. He's comfortable with corporate executives, PhDs, factory workers, down-and-outers, children, and the elderly. As transparent as glass, he is a humble man of God in the best sense of the word. How unlike so many others.

As people were in the days of the Lord Jesus, especially the Pharisees, we often want to be seen with the important people. We want others to know that, whether we're teenagers or adults, we "run with the best." We like to be with people of standing and wealth and hope others see us in the same light. Just like Hollywood stars who make a show of their generous contributions to charity on television programs, we want to be seen and honored by others. This is a very precarious place to be, and we need to carefully examine our motives.

> No one would ever question a dog's motives for wanting to be in the spotlight, but the Lord judges ours.

"The brother in humble circumstances ought to take pride in his high position," we're advised. And the text goes on to say, "But the one who is rich should take pride in his low position" (James 1:9–10). We're admonished to always have the big picture—the long-range view of things—in mind.

No one would ever question a dog's motives for wanting to be in the spotlight, but the Lord judges ours.

Scruffy

Pride goes before destruction,
a haughty spirit before a fall.
PROVERBS 16:18

Scruffy, a compilation of poodle, bull terrier, and cocker, weighs less than a robust two-month-old infant. Almost everyone and everything is bigger than Scruffy, yet Scruffy remains a scrapper. She is always ready to take up any challenge. It will come as no surprise then that she decided she could herd horses.

One day Scruffy followed her owner into the pasture. As her owner began calling and gesturing to get her horses back into the stable, Scruffy got behind the horses, barking and running. In less time than it took her owner to coax the horses into the barn, Scruffy had them running at a fast canter to get away from the nipping, noisy dog at their hooves. As fast as a flash, the three horses were inside. Quite an accomplishment for a little dog that is neither Australian shepherd nor Malinois! Scruffy trotted away with her head held high.

This scene repeated itself several times over in the course of the following months. Twelve-pound Scruffy yapping at the heels of beasts that tipped the scales at over 750 pounds each—and successfully persuading them to run into the confines of the barn at the end of the day. Scruffy's owner continued to be amazed. Scruffy was quite pleased with herself. The subjugated, proud Arabians appeared to be convinced of the power wielded by the curly-haired, gray beastie at their feet.

Or so they appeared.

One afternoon Scruffy's owner heard loud yelping coming from the pasture. Before she could get there, Scruffy came running. She showed no injury, but her eyes were full of fear and trepidation. Clearly, one of the Arabians was no longer intimidated by the would-be herder. From that day forward, Scruffy never rounded up the horses again.

Scruffy had bitten off more than she could chew.

"Even if all fall away, I will not," Peter declared when the Lord Jesus told him and the rest of the disciples that they would all desert him. The Lord corrected Peter. "But Peter insisted emphatically, 'Even if I have to die with you, I will never disown you'" (Mark 14:27–31). As good as Peter's intentions were, as convinced as he was of his loyalty, he was wrong—and the Lord Jesus was right.

The Lord taught that discipleship is costly. "Whoever comes to me I will never drive away," He said (John 6:37). But Christ also said, "No one who puts his hand to the plow and looks back is fit for service in the kingdom of God" (Luke 9:62). We are "to work out [our] salvation with fear and trembling," confident in God that He "works in [us] to will and to act according to his good purpose" (Philippians 2:12–13).

When life's glancing blows come today, our confidence in God (and not ourselves) will keep us running back into the pasture, able to meet challenges bigger than we are.

> When life's glancing blows come today, our confidence in God (and not ourselves) will keep us running.

Cassius

Likewise the tongue is a small part of the body,
but it makes great boasts.

JAMES 3:5

Where's the dog?"

The pizza deliveryman did not want to come any farther into the house. He heard the ferocious bark. A ferocious bark means a big dog. A big dog means big teeth. Big teeth make big teeth marks. Stephanie rolled her eyes and nodded with her head.

"Look down. He's at your feet."

Cassius, a miniature dachshund, barely rose to the deliveryman's ankles. And Cassius is bigger around than he is long. But his deep-throated, commanding bark more than makes up for his size—or so he thinks, as does anyone who doesn't see Cassius before hearing him. For good or ill, Cassius is emboldened by his own bark.

Cassius does not hesitate to challenge dogs two or three times his size. He is not intimidated by any dog, no matter how big. Cassius has been known to challenge two companion rottweilers who crossed his path. Cassius's next-door neighbor, a large Labrador retriever, always ends up on the loudest end of Cassius's belligerent bark. Cassius is not afraid of the big Lab. His bark crescendos to a fevered pitch whenever his husky neighbor comes into view. But the tolerant Lab is not intimidated by Cassius either. He is simply annoyed by him. The Lab walks over to Cassius, his chest and belly easily clearing the zealous, yapping, fat Cassius beneath him—and he just keeps on going.

Cassius is one dog who is all bark.

"When words are many, sin is not absent," counseled Solomon (Proverbs 10:19). A small dog barking may be amusing, annoying, or earsplitting, but the bark of a dog cannot begin to come close to creating the havoc or inflicting the pain that can be brought on by the human tongue. The tongue is untamable; it's "a restless evil, full of deadly poison." With it "we praise our Lord and

> As you go through your day, meditate on the warnings and words of the Bible about speech.

Father, and with it we curse men, who have been made in God's likeness" (James 3:8–9). With uncharacteristic understatement, James sums up his observation this way: "Out of the same mouth come praise and cursing. My brothers, this should not be" (3:10).

Though Cassius only gets wry looks from other dogs when he carries on, our speech brings more than wry looks. It can get us into trouble. "A fool's lips bring him strife," Solomon said, "and his mouth invites a beating" (Proverbs 18:6). The scriptures are replete with warnings to us about our conversation.

As you go through your day, meditate on the warnings and words of the Bible about speech. Avoid harsh words that only serve to stir up anger (Proverbs 15:1). Remember that "a deceitful tongue crushes the spirit," whereas "the tongue that brings healing is a tree of life" (15:4).

Learn from Cassius, the barking buffoon, and from Solomon, who said, "A man finds joy in giving an apt reply—and how good is a timely word!" (Proverbs 15:23).

Kiko

*"But the Lord is in his holy temple;
let all the earth be silent before him."*
HABAKKUK 2:20

Big white feet. A soft brown snout. Reddish ears and a curly tail with a white tip.

Kiko, an eight-month-old red Akita, already stands about hip high next to her owners. Her beautiful coat is more tawny in color than red. She is ready to befriend anyone and everyone. Kiko likes people, but she is very protective of Danika. Even Danika's husband must be careful when approaching his wife quickly or suddenly. Even if he playfully grabs for Danika, Kiko is ready to come to the defense of her mistress.

Like many Akitas, Kiko's barks are few and far between. She doesn't speak for a treat. She doesn't bark when there's a knock at the door. She doesn't bark at strangers. She may bark—once—on rare occasions at the sight of another animal. Even that one *woof* usually only comes out if she's startled. Otherwise, Kiko is quiet. It's not that she can't bark. She simply doesn't. She watches, she observes, and she is loyally protective. But barking is not her style.

Kiko is the strong, silent type.

Strong, silent types are rare. Everyone has an opinion.

Call-in programs fill our radio airwaves. Talk shows are abundant on both network and cable television. Chat rooms on the Internet are filled with folks wanting their voices heard. The editorial pages of our newspapers and the readers' response sections in our magazines provide us with sounding boards. Committee meetings in business, recreational activities, and church all make it clear that many of us want our opinions, thoughts, and feelings on any given subject heard and known.

Isn't it interesting that God so often encourages us to be silent? He instructs us to be silent before Him, and He not infrequently urges us to hold our peace in our dealings with others. "The Sovereign LORD has given me an instructed tongue, to know the word that sustains the weary," is our encouragement to speak forth the gospel (Isaiah 50:4). Yet we are warned as well. "Do not be quick with your mouth, do not be hasty in your heart to utter anything before God," Solomon tells us. "God is in heaven and you are on earth, so let your words be few" (Ecclesiastes 5:2). With a wry sense of humor, Solomon admonishes us: "Even a fool is thought wise if he keeps silent, and discerning if he holds his tongue" (Proverbs 17:28).

Every one of Kiko's barks, as infrequent as they are, is not wasted noise. Her rare, isolated barks speak volumes.

Similarly, since we will give an accounting to God of every word we speak, we need to weigh our words to God and to others carefully. Today "let your conversation be always full of grace, seasoned with salt" (Colossians 4:6). Salt adds flavor, retards spoilage, and acts as a preservative. Those are great qualities to be ascribed to your few words today.

Baby Eddie

Jesus called the crowd to him and said,
"Listen and understand.
What goes into a man's mouth
does not make him 'unclean,'
but what comes out of his mouth,
that is what makes him 'unclean.' "

MATTHEW 15:10–11

*B*aby Eddie is not your typical Chihuahua. He's as small as others of his kind, but he has some other peculiarities. He's black and white and willingly wears a sombrero around the house whenever Jennifer, his owner, puts it on his head. Baby Eddie, though not a baby anymore, willingly allows himself to be dressed up as a baby or as a Mexican hat dancer, even now that he's a mature ten years of age.

Baby Eddie has unusual food preferences as well: tomatoes, pickles, peanuts, olives. He even loves (and consumes) the canine gastronomical nightmare, chocolate. Baby Eddie has eaten chocolate since puppyhood. He's robust and healthy, and despite all veterinary literature to the contrary, chocolate in no way upsets his miniscule digestive tract. The only food Baby Eddie won't eat is the most Mexican of all: jalapeño peppers.

The Bible has something to say about what we put in our mouths. Meticulous detail is given to dietary restrictions in the Old Testament (see Leviticus 11). Although the Pharisees made an issue of eating practices with the Lord Jesus Christ, He was less concerned with what goes into our mouths than what comes out of them.

"Don't you see that nothing that enters a man from the outside can make him 'unclean'?" He asked. "For it doesn't go into his heart but into his stomach, and then out of his body." He went on: "What comes out of a man is what makes him 'unclean.' For from within, out of men's hearts, come evil thoughts, sexual immorality, theft, murder, adultery, greed, malice, deceit, lewdness, envy, slander, arrogance and folly. All these evils come from inside and make a man 'unclean'" (Mark 7:18–23).

What goes into our mouths is of concern if we struggle with gluttony. Solomon said, "Put a knife to your throat if you are given to gluttony" (Proverbs 23:2). But for most of us, our mouths get us into trouble because our hearts are in trouble. All the fat, salt, cholesterol, and alcohol we put into our bodies doesn't do half the damage caused by words from hearts that do not beat in accord with God's heart. "Blessed are the pure in heart," Christ said, "for they will see God" (Matthew 5:8).

If we have a problem with our speech, the Lord says to look deeper. "For out of the overflow of the heart the mouth speaks" (Matthew 12:34). Unlike Baby Eddie, who has a cast-iron stomach, we need to make sure we don't have a cast-iron heart. God's desire is that His Word be in our mouths and in our hearts (Romans 10:8).

"For it is with your heart that you believe and are justified, and it is with your mouth that you confess and are saved" (Romans 10:10).

> God's desire is that His Word be in our mouths and in our hearts (Romans 10:8).

In the Secret Place

It took my collie quite awhile to get comfortable at our new home, but as I watched where he was sniffing when we would come in, I realized that he was not nearly as eager for the place to smell like himself as he was for it to smell like me—only then would he trust he was home.

CHUCK MILLER

Boatswain

"Lord, teach us to pray."
LUKE 11:1

Eleven months old and ninety-seven pounds. Boatswain is a baby in many ways but not in body mass. He's a Newfoundland pup, growing like a weed and being taught what comes naturally—swimming.

Like other Newfies, Boatswain has been endowed by his Creator with a water-repellent coat, webbed feet, and a powerful tail that can be used as a sturdy rudder in the water. Newfies are used in water rescue all over the world. They are dropped from helicopters and ships to rescue people or products from watery graves, but before they can do all that, Newfies like Boatswain must be taught how to swim.

People who train Newfoundlands to swim are referred to as the "red-striped gang." They hold out their arms to the Newfies for directional guidance. Not all that enamored with water at first, Newfies are known for scratching up their trainers in these initial sessions. Big, frantic paws being raked down human arms leave welts, hence the name "red-striped gang." Boatswain's owner, Ace, became a member of this exclusive club during Boatswain's first summer.

None of young Boatswain's lessons have gone well so far. He flunked his puppy class because he hid under the nearest chair and refused to come out. (Boatswain, in spite of his size, is a bit timid.) Then Ace took Boatswain to his first water rescue class. Boatswain wasn't too keen on the stretch of blue water before him. He saw the benign, rhythmic, gently lapping waves of Lake Erie as puppy-munching monsters.

During one lesson, Ace swam out to the deep water and called Boatswain to him. Wanting to please, Boatswain swam as fast as his hairy paws would go. He promptly climbed on Ace's head, pushing the red-striped gang's newest member underwater.

> To be the best we can be, we must be taught as well.

It may be some time before Boatswain rescues anyone from the water.

To be the best we can be, we must be taught as well. Although we are well equipped for honorable service and duty, nothing of true worth comes naturally to us. Just as Boatswain—with webbed feet, a tail rudder, and made-to-order waterproofing—needs swimming lessons, we need some lessons, too.

Jesus' disciples, a group of Jewish men who had (presumably) prayed all their lives, said to Him, "Lord, teach us to pray," (Luke 11:1). The requesters did not say, "Teach us *how* to pray," but simply "to pray"—to do that which we might think should just happen as we seek to commune with our Maker. The Bible is replete with lessons that need to be taught: God's decrees and laws, wisdom, knowledge and good judgment, the difference between the holy and the common, self-control, and love.

And these are just a few of our life lessons!

Like Boatswain and Ace, pupil and teacher, we may be fearful of our lessons or get scratched up, but the rewards will be lasting, and even one rescue will make it all worthwhile.

Sooty

*O LORD, you have searched me and you
know me. . . . You are familiar with all my ways.*
PSALM 139:1, 3

The situation had just gone from bad to worse.

In a hurry, Ben pulled into the gas station, turned off the car, and jumped out, slamming the door behind him. All the car windows were up. Sooty, Ben's black cocker-poodle mix, jumped over the seat to get up front. She put her paws up on the door to look out adoringly at Ben.

Click.

Ben heard what happened before he saw it. Sooty's paws hit the door lock. Pink tongue lolling contentedly out of her mouth, Sooty gazed eagerly at Ben.

And there hung Ben's car keys, dangling from the steering wheel column.

Ben thought for a second. *Surely if she can lock it, she can unlock it!*

He went to the passenger side just in case. . . . No, every door was locked. Sooty bounded over to peer at her master from the passenger window. Ben went around the car, hoping to get Sooty to jump up on the armrest once more and hit UNLOCK.

"Come on, girl!" he encouraged her, tapping on the window. "Come on!"

Sooty scampered back to the other side, barking wildly and jumping up at the driver's window. This was great fun!

But Sooty's paws missed the button. That's when things deteriorated. A burly, surly truck driver pulled up behind Ben. He, too, was in a hurry. He scowled at Ben from his truck.

"I'm trying to get my dog to unlock my car!" Ben ventured to explain.

His brief explanation was understandably lost on the trucker.

There's simply no explaining some things to others. Time, circumstances, or appearances may frustrate any attempts on our part to make ourselves understood. This is not the case with God. He perceives our "thoughts from afar"; He created our inmost being (Psalm 139:2, 13). We never need to explain ourselves to God. Our motives—pure or impure—and our actions—right or wrong—are known to God. "The lamp of the LORD searches the spirit of a man; it searches out his

> We never need to explain ourselves to God.

inmost being" (Proverbs 20:27). At the end of time, what has always been true of the Lord will be made manifest for both blessing and banishment. "Not everyone who says to me, 'Lord, Lord,' will enter the kingdom of heaven, but only he who does the will of my Father who is in heaven" (Matthew 7:21). Our omniscient God wants no explanations now, nor in the future. None are needed. He sees, hears, and knows it all—the visible and the invisible, the explicable and the inexplicable.

Ben was never able to explain his predicament to the irate truck driver. The trucker slammed his vehicle into gear and went to another pump. Another filling station customer was able to unlock Ben's car with a coat hanger and a skill he picked up from. . . Well, that was not explained either.

As for Sooty? She got too excited about the game. Ben had to drive home sitting on a warm, wet seat.

Mickey

The secret things belong to the Lord our God,
but the things revealed belong to us
and to our children forever,
that we may follow all the words of this law.
DEUTERONOMY 29:29

This story took place a long time ago, back when our grandmas were just little girls.

Flossie had two prized possessions in her keeping. One was her change purse, which never had a whole lot in it. (Flossie was not a wealthy woman.) The other was her toy collie, Mickey. Mickey had no allegiance to anyone but Flossie.

In addition to her two small-sized valuables, Flossie had a number of peculiarities as well. She stored all her rubber bands on doorknobs throughout the house. Whenever her grandchildren came over, they knew just where to find a rubber band. But change for the coming ice-cream truck or penny candy at the corner store was not to be found so easily. Loose change was kept in a secret place, a place only Grandma and her dog knew. Flossie and Mickey shared a secret and guarded it carefully. Whenever Flossie needed some change, she'd tell Mickey.

"Get my purse, Mickey!"

Mickey would fetch it for her.

Only the two of them knew the secret stash spot.

For good or evil, secrets shared bind individuals together like few other things. One of the nicest compliments any of us can say of another person (or have said of us) is, "That person can keep a secret." Secrecy includes intimacy, separateness from others. In its best and purest sense, it is fragile and precious.

The Lord God has secrets. Some He chooses to keep to Himself. There are secrets of wisdom that He alone knows, and only "he knows the secrets of the heart" (Psalm 44:21). Some secrets the Creator God deigns to share with us, His created ones.

In Matthew 13:11, Jesus says that the knowledge of the secrets of the kingdom has been given to His followers. Although Job's friend spoke of God's exclusive wisdom secrets, there are some He has chosen to reveal to us. "We speak of God's secret wisdom," Paul said, "a wisdom that has been hidden and that God destined for our glory before time began" (1 Corinthians 2:7). Later he goes on to say we are "servants of Christ. . .entrusted with the secret things of God" (4:1). What a wonder this is!

Yet there is biblical warning about secrets. One day "God will judge men's secrets through Jesus Christ" (Romans 2:16). We need to be sure that our secrets are honorable before God—or that they are confessed to Him as sin. For "nothing in all creation is hidden from God's sight. Everything is uncovered and laid bare before the eyes of him to whom we must give account" (Hebrews 4:13).

Sharing a secret or two with God? Enjoy the privilege; respect the responsibility. It is an awesome thing—not at all like Mickey keeping Flossie's change purse secretly hidden in his little bed.

Sharing a secret or two with God? Enjoy the privilege; respect the responsibility.

Quigley

*"Do not store up for yourselves
treasures on earth, where moth and rust destroy,
and where thieves break in and steal.
But store up for yourselves treasures in heaven."*

Matthew 6:19–20

Quigley is a toy thief. Esther and her sister, Naomi, pamper this little shih tzu shamelessly. Quigley is given the best of food and is taken to the park for a daily walk. In inclement weather he has his own raincoat and hat. When going out, he rides in Esther's big Lincoln in a special doggy seat. Quigley travels in style, eats to contentment, and exercises to keep fit. Quigley looks innocent, but he is a thief and a robber. His sweet look and small size belie the rascal beneath the fur.

An avid ballplayer, Quigley loves to play catch. He goes over to the neighbor's and is welcomed. He will play catch until everyone tires of the game, but when he leaves, the ball goes with him. He never leaves any ball, his or another's, behind. Once Quigley plays with a toy, it becomes his. He picks it up in his mouth on the way out the door and adds it to his personal toy stash at home.

When Esther's neighbor recently had a barn sale, Quigley went over with Esther and Naomi to check out the treasures in the barn. Nonchalantly wandering about while Esther looked at the assortment of items, Quigley was eyeing his own personal selections. When he was sure no one was looking, his snooping quickly turned to snatching. He made a run for it! He grabbed item after item, running out the door with each one.

Quigley is relentlessly storing up treasures for himself.

Many of us are busy storing up treasures here on earth. When our house is full, we start accumulating more in the garage. When the stuff squeezes the cars out of the garage, we add another garage or storage shed. Eventually we have a garage sale. Then we stop at other garage sales and pick up a few items.

And so the cycle begins again.

> **Many of us are busy storing up treasures here on earth.**

Easy, isn't it, to accumulate earthly treasures? Jesus taught many parables dealing with wealth. The young son who left home ("Father, give me my share of the estate" Luke 15:12), the tale of the rich fool, and the story of the shrewd manager are just three examples. But the Lord warned that only treasures stored in heaven are safe from decay, theft, or spoilage (Matthew 6:19–20).

We must make choices. Will we squirrel away baubles and trinkets like Quigley the toy thief, or will we heed the Lord's admonishment?

"Provide purses for yourselves that will not wear out, a treasure in heaven that will not be exhausted. . . . For where your treasure is, there your heart will be also" (Luke 12:33–34).

Bathtub Buffy

Hide me in the shadow of your wings.
PSALM 17:8

Some dogs enjoy being groomed. Buffy is not one of those dogs.

Maggie's brown-and-white cocker spaniel knows the sound of the groom-mobile. Whenever Buffy hears or sees the approach of her grooming service on wheels, she does her disappearing act. The groomer knows he's not one of Buffy's favorite people, and he, too, puts off the inevitable as long as he can. He always does Maggie's other dog first. When Buffy's time comes, he sighs and tells Maggie: "Time to get the tow truck to drag Buffy out here."

In all her years of trying to avoid getting spruced up, Buffy has gotten quite creative at finding hiding places. But the house is small, and she is an indoor dog; she cannot hide for long. The one time she almost succeeded in remaining a scruffy Buffy, she found the perfect hiding spot. She jumped in the bathtub and hid behind the shower curtain—no small feat for a little dog like Buffy. But Maggie managed to find her, and Buffy got beautified in spite of herself. As Buffy was washed, dried, combed, and buffed to a shine, one phrase may have been passing through her mind: *Nowhere to run, nowhere to hide.*

Want to run and hide some days? Maybe today?

Throughout the Bible we have accounts of people just like us, people who wanted to run to God and hide or find a place of hiding in God. David, the poet-warrior who became king, asked God to hide him as a bird hides her young under her wings. In another psalm David asked God to hide him "from the conspiracy of the wicked, from that noisy crowd of evildoers" (Psalm 64:2). Perhaps this is a prayer you ask for your children or grandchildren. It is a comfort to know that we can call on God to provide us a hiding place when it is needed.

But what if we want to hide from God? The Bible speaks of those who have tried to hide from Him whose "eyes. . .range throughout the earth" (2 Chronicles 16:9). Just as is true for Buffy, there is no place to run or hide from God. As one of our English poets of long ago said, God is the great hound of heaven. He will find us every time. How much better it is to hide *in* Him than to try to hide *from* Him. For "nothing in all creation is hidden from God's sight" (Hebrews 4:13).

> It is a comfort to know that we can call on God to provide us a hiding place when it is needed.

Buffy can no longer hide in the bathtub. Age and weight have made scaling the edge of the tub an impossible task—just as it is impossible for us to hide from God. Yet our encouragement remains in the rest of that verse from 2 Chronicles: "For the eyes of the LORD range throughout the earth to strengthen those whose hearts are fully committed to him" (16:9).

145

Shadow

When Jesus heard this, he was amazed at him, and turning to the crowd following him, he said, "I tell you, I have not found such great faith even in Israel."

LUKE 7:9

I kept waiting for her to explode or vomit."

Those were Mischel's words about her ninety-plus-pound German shepherd, Shadow. Mischel spent an entire day baking Christmas cutout cookies. After mixing, baking, and frosting twelve dozen cookies, she left them on the kitchen table for the night. Once the icing had hardened, she would put them into containers the next day.

When Mischel went to the kitchen the next morning, there was a trail of cookie crumbs and sugar sprinkles from table to chair to the place where Shadow always eats her doggy treats. There sat Shadow, heavier than she had been the night before. She had eaten about four dozen iced and sprinkled sugar cookies. It's hard to believe, but Shadow never got sick, went into a diabetic coma, or exploded. And she still loves Christmas cutout cookies!

Mischel and her family acquired Shadow after she failed her cadet training at the police academy. The reason she failed? Shadow is terrified of loud noises. She shakes uncontrollably when it thunders. She has to be sedated every year on July 4. Only heaven knows what she'd do if she ever heard a gunshot. As big and as intimidating as she may appear, Shadow is just a fainthearted cookie-holic. She's not your typical German shepherd.

Mischel can't trust Shadow around Christmas cookies. She can't depend on her to protect the children during a thunderstorm. Shadow is not what anyone expects a burly German shepherd to be.

Shadow is just a big marshmallow with fur and a sweet tooth.

There are two times in scripture where the Lord Jesus Christ is described as amazed. He was amazed ("marvelled" in the KJV) at the great faith of the centurion who believed Jesus only had to speak a

> Now that the Lord Jesus Christ has ascended to heaven, He is "far above all rule and authority, power and dominion" (Ephesians 1:21).

word for his request to be accomplished (Matthew 8:10). The Lord was amazed to find such faith not in an Israelite, but in a Gentile. The other time Jesus marveled—when the response He received was not what He expected—was on a visit to his hometown. Few could believe that one of their own, a local boy, had the credentials to teach in the synagogue. The Lord Jesus was not what they expected, any more than their indifferent response to Him was what He expected. The Lord "was amazed at their lack of faith" (see Mark 6:1–6).

Now that the Lord Jesus Christ has ascended to

heaven, He is "far above all rule and authority, power and dominion" (Ephesians 1:21). He is beyond amazement. He looks at the heart and knows the thoughts of people. He knows us inside and out—not what we might appear to be to others, but who and what we truly are.

Queenie

There is a friend who sticks closer than a brother.
PROVERBS 18:24

Todd and his shepherd-collie mix, Queenie, have grown up together. They live in a small town where everyone knows everyone else. When Todd is out with his dog, the neighbors recognize both of them and know them by name. As a little guy who would get into his play tractor and pedal his way over to Grandma's, Todd was constantly under Queenie's protective surveillance. Todd's mom would call her mother to tell her Todd and Queenie were on their way over to visit. Grandma would watch for them, but she never feared for them. Queenie walked patiently alongside Todd and his tractor. No one was allowed in the tight space between them. Queenie saw to that. Once Todd entered grade school, however, he left his pedal-powered tractor behind him to ride the school bus.

Queenie can't go to school, but she watches Todd leave every morning from the front porch. She remains there all day, five days a week, fair weather and foul, until her young charge comes home. When Todd comes home from school and greets his dog with a pat on the head, they are again inseparable. Weekends, summers, and breaks from school provide Todd and Queenie with ample time to play or get into mischief. Fiercely protective of Todd, Queenie is constantly at his side. The friendship between

> **Whether you've been fortunate to have a lifelong friend here on earth or not, there is One who can be your Friend for this life and the next.**

this dog and her boy is deep and true.

How rare it is to find deep friendships that span years, differences, and all the changes that come with life. Dorothy and Marjorie are two women, both now in their eighties, who have been friends since they were in kindergarten. Their friendship has lasted through the turbulence of youth, the mayhem of rearing young ones, and the sorrows of illness and death. Their unique bond of friendship does not need common blood or heritage.

Perhaps you've never been fortunate enough to have such a friend. Perhaps distance, differences of opinion or worldview, the business of life, or the enemy death severed the thread you both thought unbreakable. It may be that you've never allowed yourself to get that close to anyone. That kind of vulnerability is too great a risk for you to take.

Whether you've been fortunate to have a lifelong friend here on earth or not, there is One who can be your Friend for this life and the next. He never fails; He "sticks closer than a brother." Desertion is not in His vocabulary, and He loves you above all you can imagine. "A friend loves at all times," we're told (Proverbs 17:17), and this Friend of sinners has already gone so far as to lay down His life for you, me, and all the world.

Like Queenie walking beside Todd on his little red tractor, no thing and no person can come between us and this Friend, Jesus, who has chosen us for Himself.

Lulu

*"Those who cling to worthless idols
forfeit the grace that could be theirs."*
JONAH 2:8

Lulu has an obsession.

Lulu, a curly-tailed, long-haired Pomeranian puff ball of a dog, will not lay aside or lay down her prize for love nor money. Lulu clings to her bright-green tennis ball with the tenacity of a pit bull. She carries it around the house when she's awake. If she goes outside for any reason, her tennis ball is securely in her mouth. When she sleeps, the ball is nestled protectively between her two front legs. Lulu sets her tennis ball down to eat, but that's it, and that's not for long. There is no separating Lulu and her ball.

Except when the green is gone.

There comes a point when Lois, Lulu's owner, must dispense with the old and give Lulu a new tennis ball. The ball, which has seen better days, becomes disgusting. So Lois dispenses with the sodden, deformed object that is Lulu's exclusive, precious icon.

This is major trauma for neurotic Lulu. She whines and carries on for days, suspiciously eyeing the new ball that Lois puts down for her. Buffy, Lulu's companion, cannot understand her playmate's woebegone whimpering. Lulu goes to pieces, mourning the loss of her inconsequential (but to her, cherished) tennis ball. That ball is vitally important to Lulu. She is lost without it.

Some of the hardest, in-your-face verses in the Bible have to do with idol worship. The Lord, the Maker of all, has no patience with, nor does He make allowances for, those who cling to other gods. God's very first commandment is "You shall have no other gods before me." If we miss or overlook the first commandment, the Lord drives home His point even further with the second commandment: "You shall not make for yourself an idol in the form of anything" (Exodus 20:3–4). To value anything or anyone above the Invaluable One is to invite disaster and judgment on our own heads.

Oh, to see and understand the importance of giving to God the glory due Him alone! Do we hear the heart of the Father when He asks, "If I am a father, where is the honor due me? If I am a master, where is the respect due me?" (Malachi 1:6). Nothing is to usurp the place of the Lord God Almighty in our lives.

> Oh, to see and understand the importance of giving to God the glory due Him alone!

The Lord Jesus said it this way: "Love the Lord your God with all your heart and with all your soul and with all your mind" (Matthew 22:37). It's all or none when it comes to committing ourselves to the One who made us and loves us. We're to hold our confidence in Christ firmly to the end and to "hold firmly to the faith we profess" so that we can "receive mercy and find grace to help us in our time of need" (Hebrews 4:14, 16).

It's time to let go of the fuzzless tennis ball and cling to the real prize.

ANOTHER Jake

Turn my eyes away from worthless things;
preserve my life according to your word.

PSALM 119:37

Kaed would have to confess: it's all her fault.

Her toy fox terrier, now eight years old (a mature dog by anyone's measure), has a dependency that would be pitiful even if Jake were a child and not a dog. Jake is a pacifier-dependent fully grown dog. Jake is hooked on his binky.

When he was a puppy, he was dressed up—just for fun—in baby doll clothes and given a pacifier. Even then he didn't suck on the thing, but he held it in his mouth for pictures. Then he kept it in his mouth when there was no camera around. Soon he was walking around with the pacifier in his mouth. Eight years later, Jake is still carrying a baby pacifier around the house. He's hooked. On occasion, he'll forget about the pacifier for a while, but before long, it's back in his mouth. Kaed's other dogs wouldn't think of touching, sniffing, or carting around Jake's pacifier.

The worthless pacifier is Jake's prized possession. He walks around casually on his skinny toothpick legs and has no idea how ridiculous he looks.

"Turn my eyes away from worthless things," the psalmist prayed (Psalm 119:37). In the context of the Bible's longest song, the songwriter asked God to keep him focused on the important. Just prior to these words, he besought God in a number of areas having to do with personal conduct. "Teach me, O LORD, to follow your decrees," he said. "Turn my heart toward your statutes and not toward selfish gain" (119:33, 36). How we need to repeat the words of the psalmist's prayer. How much more we need to practice them.

> How well and quickly we respond to the loud, insistent cry of the urgent—yet often miss the important details that are barely perceptible whispers.

How well and quickly we respond to the loud, insistent cry of the urgent—yet often miss the important details that are barely perceptible whispers. Before long, we've filled up our lives with overtime at work to buy worthless things. Or we've spent countless days giving time and attention to matters of little import from heaven's eternal perspective. "Teach us to number our days aright," Moses said, "that we may gain a heart of wisdom" (Psalm 90:12). Even Moses, who is called "the man of God" in the title of this psalm, knew how easy it is to get absorbed by the worthless. We, too, need to ask the Lord for discernment. We need to be wary of the lure of, or our attachment to, worthless things.

Remember Jake, a grown dog with no sucking reflex, who holds a pacifier resolutely between his teeth.

Bambi and Chad

Accept him whose faith is weak,
without passing judgment on disputable matters.
ROMANS 14:1

Patty has been fortunate in that she has had two good, compliant dogs in her life. Bambi was a terrier mix whose only claim to fame was that he didn't swim. He floated. It might have been that Bambi had put on a few pounds too many as he got older, but he never doggy-paddled his way around any body of water. A trip to the beach meant floating around effortlessly in the surf, content to be (as happened on one occasion) the photo focus of tourists from Europe who found the sight one of their most entertaining in the United States.

Chad, the dog Patty has now, is a black Labrador mix. A good-sized dog with floppy ears, a friendly face, and a white tip on the end of his tail, Chad was fourteen years old when he had to learn to share Patty's attention with a new family member, a baby girl. Suddenly, Chad is not the family baby. He's a big brother. Unlike some dogs, Chad has no jealousy toward the new baby. He is willing to share his owners' attention and love with the baby.

Both Bambi and Chad learned to go with the flow.

We, too, have to know when to be rigid and when to be flexible. We are to be rigid and inflexible in matters of holiness and love. "Be holy" is an Old Testament command reiterated in the New (Leviticus 11:44–45; 2 Timothy 1:9). Love defines us as Christ followers. As the blind man healed by the Lord Jesus Christ did, we are to worship God and God alone. In these areas and some others, there is no room for deviation or laxity.

Most of chapters 14 and 15 in the book of Romans and chapters 8 to 10 in 1 Corinthians are dedicated to disputable matters, those things that call for love and discretion. In the early Christian church, one area of contention had to do with meat purchased from pagan temples. Other issues from the early church overlap into our present day: Should those in full-time ministry have a secular job to cover expenses? Should Christians be vegetarians?

> We, too, have to know when to be rigid and when to be flexible.

Some of today's issues did not confront the early Christians. Should we send our children to a public school or a Christian school? Should we homeschool our children? Do we pad the church pews or not? Clearly, disputable matters are here to stay.

Fortunately, the answers to all these questions come down to a few basic principles given right in the Word of God: "Therefore let us stop passing judgment on one another. Instead, make up your mind not to put any stumbling block or obstacle in your brother's way" (Romans 14:13). "So whatever you believe about these things keep between yourself and God" (14:22).

Avoid majoring on the minors. Like Chad and Bambi, sometimes we need to go with the flow.

Living the Truth

*Jesus, I thought, was watching how
I witnessed to my neighbors,
and He was;
Jesus, I thought, was watching how
I raised my children, and He was;
Jesus, I thought, was watching how
honest I was at work, and He was.
How was I to know that what He was
scrutinizing—this God of little
things—was how I treat my collie.*

CHUCK MILLER

Max

*"I am a woman who is deeply troubled. . . .
I was pouring out my soul to the LORD."*
1 SAMUEL 1:15

Max is a fifty-plus-pound bull terrier and Labrador mix who doesn't back down from a challenge. If Max doesn't have a challenge, he looks for one.

When Max arrived on the farm, he set about investigating his new home. In addition to the already present assortment of dogs and cats, there were also some horses. Max had not seen a horse before, except on television, perhaps. *Hmm.* He went over to have a closer look.

Max decided right then he didn't like horses, or he decided they presented a formidable challenge—or both. Whatever the case, Max's ears went up. He sized up the horses from his position just outside the corral. He was going to let these steeds know he was boss. He was taking charge. All four feet planted, Max began his fiercest, most assertive barking.

Immediately, two of the horses ran to a far corner of the pasture. They recognized authority and challenge when they heard it. They decided they were not up to the challenge. Not the youngest horse, however. She barely looked up. Indeed, she continued to contentedly munch on the grass at her feet, barely acknowledging the barking dog before her.

Max continued to bark.

Horse continued her snack. She flattened her ears ever so slightly against her head.

Max hunkered down on his front feet. His pitch increased; his barking intensified.

Horse's ears lay flatter still. She kept eating. Her eyes, looking covertly at the noisy dog from beneath half-closed lids, narrowed.

Max hunkered down farther, his tail upright. Louder still, resonating across the ranch, the persistent barking increased in rapidity, ferocity, and intensity.

That did it. Horse charged the irritating dog!

In 1 Samuel 1, Hannah is presented as a godly woman, bitter of soul. She longed for a child; she prayed for a child; but no child came. Her husband's other wife, Peninnah, had many children. Peninnah, Hannah's rival, kept provoking her.

We, too, may be irritated by people or circumstances over which we have no control. Like Hannah, we weep; we lose our appetite; we pray. Hannah's prayer for a child was answered, but the irritant, Peninnah, remained. She did not go away when Hannah's children were born. Paul the apostle begged God to take away the thorn in his flesh. Instead, God gave him the grace to live with it instead of the relief of living without it (2 Corinthians 12:7–10).

The dog-horse challenge was a standoff: Max on one

side of the fence, Horse on the other. Max didn't back down; he kept barking. Horse turned, kicked dirt on him, and trotted away, her head held high.

> **Pray. Wait on God.**

If you are beleaguered by an irritant, remember Hannah and Paul, Horse and Max. Pray. Wait on God. The answer may not come in the form you expect, but God is faithful to answer.

Dakota and Cheyenne

"If I am a father, where is the honor due me?
If I am a master, where is the respect due me?"
says the LORD Almighty.
MALACHI 1:6

*B*aby Number One is on the way. Liz and her husband are looking forward to parenting with an understandable mix of expectancy, anticipation, and apprehension. What will it be like having this precious new life to love and provide for? There's only so much advice that can be taken in and so many books one can read. Yet Liz thinks they may have an edge as they anticipate being parents. They have two dogs.

Dakota, a shepherd-collie mix, and Cheyenne, a black Labrador, have been teaching Liz and her husband a little something about parenting for several years. Devotion and love are two things Dakota and Cheyenne have demonstrated and taught Liz through good and hard times. Whether it's waking up in the morning and having the two of them jump up to rouse her out of bed or whether it's Dakota standing guard outside Liz's room, both dogs add warmth, love, and joy to life daily. When Liz is feeling down, Dakota and Cheyenne manage to do some silly stunt that gets her laughing. But dog ownership isn't all fun and games, hugs and cuddle sessions.

When Liz gets up in the morning, she must feed Dakota and Cheyenne before she puts a thing in her own mouth. Even if she's feeling lousy and as if she's fifteen months pregnant, Liz still has to pick up after her two charges. When Dakota and Cheyenne are being good, they are very good. But when they're being bad—let's just say it's possible to be very bad when they have eight paws, a truckload of fur, and over one hundred pounds between the two of them.

Liz has taught her two dogs a lot, but along the way, Cheyenne and Dakota have been doing some teaching of their own. Liz can rest her hand on her swelling abdomen and almost hear her dogs' encouragement.

The real thing's coming, Mom! We're helping you get ready!

> **Before God made each of us, He knew us and loved us.**

One of the most heartrending passages in the Old Testament is God's series of questions to His people in the book of Malachi. "If I am a father," He asks (and He is Father—Progenitor—of all), "where is the honor due me?" (Malachi 1:6). His question reverberates with pain. Before God made each of us, He knew us and loved us. God was and is the perfect Parent, yet His first children flagrantly disobeyed Him, and we have been doing so ever since. But His love remains constant, and the Word says, "The LORD takes delight in his people" (Psalm 149:4).

Whether we have adoring pets or not, whether we are

blessed with children or not, the Lord God teaches by word and confirms by demonstration His pure parental love for us: unrivaled, unconditional, and sacrificial, even if His love is left painfully unrequited.

Lassie

*Can the Ethiopian change his skin
or the leopard its spots?
Neither can you do good
who are accustomed to doing evil.*

JEREMIAH 13:23

*A*s a little girl, Lisa's favorite television program was *Lassie*. Lassie and her little owner, Timmy, were Lisa's heroes. Lisa wanted her own Lassie.

Ever have a daughter or son beg relentlessly for a pet? Lisa hounded (you might say) her parents for months for her own collie. John and his wife, both animal lovers, finally decided the time had come. They thought Lisa was old enough and responsible enough to have her own dog. They bought and brought home Lisa's new dog.

Thrilled is an inadequate adjective for describing Lisa's reaction to her new pet. She smothered the young puppy with hugs and kisses. She named her (what else?) Lassie. The young puppy was a black collie with sable trim about her face, a white underbelly, and a natural white collar. Lisa wasn't quite sure why she didn't look exactly like the Lassie of television fame, but she loved her new puppy all the same.

"She's a puppy, honey," her dad told her. "She'll grow and change a lot, just like a baby."

That contented Lisa for a while. Not infrequently she assigned her father to play the role of Timmy. The three of them would act out their own untelevised *Lassie* program. But Lisa kept asking, "When is Lassie going to look like the TV Lassie?"

Finally, John explained to Lisa that their Lassie would never look exactly like the Lassie on television. Lisa was stunned.

"You mean all her black hair isn't going to fall out? She'll never be brown and white like the real Lassie?"

As much as Lisa wanted her Lassie to look like the famous collie, it would never happen. Her Lassie was a tricolor collie. Lisa's Lassie could no more turn brown than a leopard can change its spots.

God's prophet Jeremiah told the Israelites that they were accustomed to doing the wrong thing. They were incapable of doing right. Solomon wrote, "For as he thinketh in his heart, so is he" (Proverbs 23:7 KJV). The Lord Jesus Christ told us we recognize people by how they live—not by what they say. "A good tree cannot bear bad fruit, and a bad tree cannot bear good fruit. . . . Thus, by their fruit you will recognize them" (Matthew 7:18, 20).

Does someone come to your mind when you think on any of these verses, someone you want to believe the best of, yet who continually disappoints you with godless ways? You want this person to change his spots, but at the same time, you know that he cannot. We all are incapable of changing our nature.

But God Almighty is in the business of changing hearts. This change is so dramatic that He calls us a "new creation" (2 Corinthians 5:17). Thankfully, He can remove our hearts of stone and give us pliable hearts of flesh (Ezekiel 11:19).

> **We all are incapable of changing our nature. But God Almighty is in the business of changing hearts.**

Casey

When Jesus rose early on the first day of the week,
he appeared first to Mary Magdalene,
out of whom he had driven seven demons.

MARK 16:9

Casey had been abused. The veterinarian who examined him shook his head. Who might he call to take this poor creature and give him a good home? He thought of a couple, Al and Sue, who had had dogs throughout their lives. He knew if anyone could nurse Casey back to health, it would be Al and Sue. He gave them a call and explained Casey's situation. Al told him to bring Casey over.

When the vet brought Casey to Al and Sue, the puppy was a sorry compilation of infection, worms, and protruding ribs. At a mere five months, his life had been anything but happy. Once in the house, however, Casey went right to Al. He sensed security from the big man and was ready to befriend anyone who did not treat him like a dog, as the crude expression says it. For their part, Al and Sue knew Casey was the dog for them. Slowly but surely, Casey began to thrive in his new home. He was bathed in TLC. He eventually sprouted to his current robust sixty pounds.

On rare occasions Casey still cowers for no apparent reason, but he is gentle, loving, and sensitive. When someone comes to the door, Casey barks. Once. Otherwise, he quietly, contentedly goes about his happy life in his happy home. He loves the grandkids. Whenever more than one of them comes over, Casey instinctively knows which child needs an extra dose of affection. That grandchild is the one who then receives his undivided attention. He is easily Grandpa and Grandma's third pair of watchful eyes.

Delivered from terror and encompassed by love, Casey now ministers to others.

Mary Magdalene is mentioned in every Gospel account. Both John Mark and Luke tell us that Jesus had cast seven demons out of her. Every Gospel account identifies her as the first one at the tomb of the Lord Jesus on Resurrection Sunday. We know three other things about this remarkable woman. She was a follower of the Lord Jesus Christ and cared for His needs. She helped support Him out of her own resources, and she was near Him as He hung on the cross. Jesus had delivered Mary of Magdala from a life of demon terror. In return, she supported Him whenever, wherever, and however she could.

Demons abuse those in whom they take up residence. Sadly, sometimes people abuse animals who reside with them. How marvelous it is that God can break those chains of terror and victimization. Sometimes it is our privilege to do for a helpless animal what the Lord Christ

> What a blessing we see when a transformed pet or person ministers in kind and genuine ways to others.

does for the helpless human. What a blessing we see when a transformed pet or person ministers in kind and genuine ways to others. It is beauty for ashes, gladness instead of mourning, praise instead of despair (Isaiah 61:3).

Captain Black

*"Lord, how many times shall I forgive my brother
when he sins against me?
Up to seven times?"
Jesus answered, "I tell you,
not seven times,
but seventy-seven times."*
MATTHEW 18:21–22

Tim describes Captain Black as a schnoodle, half schnauzer and half poodle. Captain is affectionate. His favorite spot is on Tim's chest. Captain Black's most unique feature? He has the proverbial nine lives of a cat.

First, Captain Black fell off a roof. Tim ran to his rescue. Captain Black survived his fall without so much as a broken bone. Captain Black ingested some chicken bones once. Poultry bones are especially dangerous for dogs. Tim had to take his dog to the veterinarian to have a special procedure done in order for the dog to survive that dietary faux pas, but Captain Black did make a full recovery.

Captain Black's closest call to death came one day when he and Tim were outside. One minute Captain Black was nosing his way around the yard, the next Tim saw him collapse and fall on his side. Rushing over to his little dog,

Tim found him choking on some rose vines. Tim had to move quickly; there was no time to drive to the vet's. Tim pulled the thorny vines out of Captain Black's throat. Shaken but alive, Captain Black once again bounced back from a near-death experience. For at least the third time in his life, Captain Black was saved yet again by his loving master, Tim.

How many times will Tim save his dog from death? "Up to seven times?"

Because of his love for his dog, Tim will save him as often as is necessary. Not once has Tim reprimanded his dog with, "Why did you go and do something like this again?" Tim overlooks Captain Black's poor judgment.

Sometimes when others sin against us, it's not intentional. Sometimes, of course, it is. Either way, when they come seeking forgiveness, God says we are to forgive like He forgives. He lavishes forgiveness upon us who, in no way, can make it right or repay our debt to Him. We sin against God daily. When we confess our sin, He forgives us—daily. Likewise, we are to forgive others who cannot undo what they have said or done. We are to lavish forgiveness on others.

The Lord is very forthright about this. "Forgive your brother from your heart," He commands us (Matthew 18:35). When Stephen, the first recorded Christian martyr, was stoned to death, he forgave his unrepentant executioners. The Lord Jesus, who had died, risen, and was sitting at the right hand of God, stood to cheer on Stephen (Acts 7:54–60) as he made his confession and forgave those who put him to death.

Just as Tim repeatedly saved the life of his dog out of love for him, we need to practice acts of repetitive love toward others. We are to forgive others, just as in Christ God forgave us.

> **We are to forgive others, just as in Christ God forgave us.**

Elizabeth and Edgar

Brothers, think of what you were when you were called.
Not many of you were wise by human standards;
not many were influential; not many were of noble birth.
1 CORINTHIANS 1:26

Elizabeth, a collie, had been beaten—and disposed of—for chewing on her owner's sofa. Edgar, a mixed terrier, developed a malignant pituitary tumor that eventually took his life, despite tender care. These dogs are just some of the dogs Carol has rescued and cared for over the years.

Carol takes dogs that no one else will take. She picks up abandoned, sickly strays. She nurses to health rejected puppy-mill dogs, who are bred for profit but unsold. Carol has often done only what could be done: make a suffering dog's last days as painless as possible. A registered nurse by profession, Carol has spent untold hours providing nursing care for the numerous ailing or damaged dogs she's taken in. She's done everything from administering antibiotics to intravenous chemotherapy for her beloved pets. She's applied eye salve every four hours around the clock for dogs with tear-duct problems. She's sustained dogs with tube feedings every three hours. After Elizabeth, the abused collie, had her first stroke, Carol and her husband taught her how to walk again.

Carol has never been one to seek out finely bred dogs or the dogs that would take Best of Show. Her dogs are the ones who have been abused, neglected, or abandoned. Many of her dogs are not loving or lovable. It takes patience over the long haul before a previously abused dog will acquiesce to one solitary, gentle touch of Carol's hand.

Carol doesn't do what she does for accolades or awards. Her ministrations to dogs such as Elizabeth and Edgar are done from the best source of motivation: a heart of love.

The Old Testament prophets of God were, by and large, a motley crew. They did weird things like letting birds feed them. They shaved (or never shaved) their heads. When Christ came to earth, His arrival wasn't announced to the political and religious leaders of His day. Only a handful of stargazers and some squalid shepherds were cognizant of the world's single most important birth. The apostle Paul writes that God chooses the foolish, weak, lowly, despised of the world (1 Corinthians 1:27–28).

> Jesus encourages us to think and act like His Father—to ignore present gratification.

Jesus encourages us to think and act like His Father—to ignore present gratification. "When you give a luncheon or dinner,'" He said, "'do not invite your friends. . .or your rich neighbors; if you do, they may invite you back and so you will be repaid. But when you give a banquet, invite the poor, the crippled, the lame, the blind, and you will be blessed" (Luke 14:12–14).

Easy words to acknowledge, but not so easy to live—whether we're extending that hospitality to an abandoned dog or a hapless human.

Merlin-Thomas and Bailey

The boys grew up,
and Esau became a skillful hunter,
a man of the open country,
while Jacob was a quiet man,
staying among the tents.
GENESIS 25:27

*J*ennifer's dogs, Merlin-Thomas and Bailey, are as unalike as Jacob and Esau. Merlin-Thomas, "T" for short, is a black Labrador mix. Bailey is a reddish golden retriever. T has a problem with attitude. He thinks the place for dogs—for him anyway—is anywhere a human happens to be sitting. If Jennifer is on the sofa or her bed, that's the spot T wants to be. He cries and carries on until he gets the MVP (Most Valuable Place). Jennifer either has to move or endure T's whimpering, whining, and woebegone protest. T is only interested in displacing Jennifer for his own comfort and convenience.

Bailey has no such obsession with Jennifer's furniture. Bailey does have an obsession with Jennifer. Bailey doesn't want to be alone. He enjoys touch. He always manages to snuggle up to Jennifer, no matter what she's doing. He either sticks his nose under her hand or plants his head firmly against her leg. Bailey is like static cling when it comes to Jennifer. If she's around, Bailey is there, nuzzling his owner with rapt adoration.

T wants what's Jennifer's. Bailey just wants Jennifer.

Throughout the Bible we have accounts of siblings who are strikingly different. Abel kept flocks and did things God's way. Cain worked the soil and did things his own way. Simon Peter was forever getting himself in trouble for what he said. Andrew, his brother, only spoke twice in scripture. The most important instance that is recorded for us are his words to Peter: "We have found the Messiah" (John 1:41).

Two of scripture's most famous siblings are Mary and her sister, Martha. Like T, Martha was concerned about the house. Mary, like Bailey, wanted to be close to the One who came into the house. In his customary, tender-yet-direct way, the Lord Jesus replied to a whining Martha, "You are worried and upset about many things, but only one thing is needed. Mary has chosen what is better, and it will not be taken away from her" (Luke 10:41–42).

Sandi has the gift of hospitality. People feel welcome in her home. By example, Sandi teaches an important lesson to all on the receiving end of her generosity. When the food is eaten and the time comes to sit around and fellowship, she has two words for the remaining mess: "Leave it."

Sandi knows the dirty dishes won't magically disappear. She knows the countertops won't self-clean. But she also knows when friends come together it's time to get close again. Those times are too rare, too precious,

> In your contacts with the Lord and with people today, be like Bailey, Mary, and Sandi. Choose what is better.

too brief in our busy culture to take second place to the stack of dishes or the clutter in the kitchen.

In your contacts with the Lord and with people today, be like Bailey, Mary, and Sandi. Choose what is better.

Cinnamon

"Who despises the day of small things?"

ZECHARIAH 4:10

Miniature dachshunds are notorious for congenital back problems, and Cinnamon, as she got older, was no exception. In her younger days, the family favorite could keep up easily with the three children. But as the years passed, Ray and his family started to notice that Cinnamon hesitated to jump down from the couch. Then she had problems navigating the stairs. Soon she began to drag one foot. Ray took his aging pet to the vet.

What Ray and his wife feared had happened. Cinnamon had developed the anomaly common to her breed. An operation for a bad disk was scheduled. Following intricate surgery and a prolonged hospitalization, Cinnamon was ready to come home.

The hard work began for Ray. Not only did Ray have to assist Cinnamon with her activities of daily living, as they're called in medical jargon, but he had to begin her rehabilitation. Cinnamon had to learn how to walk all over again. This was done by filling the bathtub with water and then suspending Cinnamon so her feet would not touch bottom. She would move and strengthen her little legs before putting any weight on them. Her rehabilitation was a long and tedious, but necessary, process. Ray did it faithfully with Cinnamon every day for weeks, for

Cinnamon's benefit, to restore her to normal, and for his children's benefit, who loved her like a sister.

So much of life is lived in the little things. Small kindnesses that go unnoticed; tender touches that linger only in memory. Things we hardly thought about in our early adult years come back to us when we have our own children. We seek to do for our children as our moms and dads did for us. Maybe they took us to a not-too-distant hotel for one night of swimming in the hotel pool and staying in a new bedroom. They taught us how to bait a hook or possibly how to swing a bat. They bought us a new pet or gently aided the one we had back to health.

The Lord Jesus told a parable about a dishonest manager. At its conclusion He said, "Whoever can be trusted with very little can also be trusted with much" (Luke 16:10). The widow in Zarephath had only a handful of flour and a little oil in a jug, yet because of her generosity and God's promise, she fed herself, her son, and the prophet Elijah through the long drought (1 Kings 17:7–16). A chapter later, a "cloud as small as a man's hand" heralds the coming deluge (18:44–45). There are "four things on earth [that] are small, yet they are extremely wise" (Proverbs 30:24).

> God takes note of little things.

Little kindnesses: teaching a dog to walk, a boy to bat. Little responsibilities: handling money wisely, sharing what little food you have. Little wonders: a small cloud promising a drought's end, ants planning ahead.

God takes note of little things.

Poochie

"But my mouth would encourage you;
comfort from my lips would bring you relief."

Job 16:5

*B*abysitting is fraught with hazards.

Lindy was watching her little nephew. She was new to babysitting. Being the baby of the family herself, Lindy never had to care for younger siblings. She was understandably nervous about this first job. Bobby was still an infant, but he crawled around the house, happily entertaining himself under Lindy's watchful eyes. Lindy was also babysitting Poochie, her brother's new dog. Poochie was a dachshund puppy, hardly bigger than Bobby.

The evening had gone quite smoothly when Lindy noticed Bobby chewing on something. She ran to get whatever was in Bobby's mouth out of it. She was horrified to find loose teeth.

What had he done? Had he fallen and she didn't know it? There was no blood or bruising, but Lindy feared Bobby had hurt himself in some way and knocked teeth out in the process! How would she ever tell her brother? Bobby didn't appear injured, but Lindy dreaded her brother's return.

Bobby's parents had not been home but a few minutes when Lindy confessed her negligence. She opened her hand to show her brother the teeth. To Lindy's surprise (and profound relief), Bobby's father roared with laughter.

"Those aren't Bobby's teeth! Poochie is losing his baby teeth!"

Years ago an antacid commercial asked, "How do you spell 'relief'?" Relief comes in so many forms. It may come with three words: "There's no cancer." It might be a son returning—hours past curfew—but returning nonetheless. Perhaps the relief is allergy medication. Relief from worry, pain, or unease is always a welcome friend.

God, too, speaks of relief. Sometimes He gives relief; at other times He withholds it. When the Israelites asked God for a king, He gave them their request, but he tempered it with a warning. "When that day comes, you will cry out for relief from the king you have chosen, and the LORD will not answer you in that day" (1 Samuel 8:18). Paul told the Thessalonians that their suffering had a limit. "God is just," he wrote. "He will pay back trouble to those who trouble you and give relief to you who are troubled" (2 Thessalonians 1:6–7).

Feeling like you need some relief today? Find it from the psalmist's source: "Blessed is the man you discipline, O LORD. . .you grant him relief from days of trouble" (Psalm 94:12–13).

Relief might be as small a thing as Poochie's baby

teeth; it may be as big a thing as being delivered from a mortal enemy. Whatever the case, call on God for relief. "Answer me when I call to you, O my righteous God. Give me relief from my distress; be merciful to me and hear my prayer" (Psalm 4:1).

> Whatever the case, call on God for relief.

Having prayed, place those puppy teeth into the hand of your loving Father and utter a sigh of relief.

ANOTHER Casey

Get Mark and bring him with you,
because he is helpful to me in my ministry.

2 TIMOTHY 4:11

Casey is a five-year-old has-been. The beautiful golden retriever, once a trained guide dog, lost his position and status as a guide for the blind. Through no fault of his own, Casey was aimlessly leading his mistress through the hot streets of a Texas town. Overexposed to the hot Texas sun, Casey suffered a heatstroke. Disoriented, he was not able to guide his mistress. The damages to Casey's abilities as a guide dog were irreversible. He was sold to a sighted person.

Rosalie, her husband, and their three boys have learned some other things about Casey since he joined their family. Casey is still a supersmart dog. He learned how to use his own private doggy door in one session. Although Casey still tends to be a one-woman dog (he is clearly partial to Rosalie), he learns quickly and is obedient. But Casey has a lazy streak.

When it's suppertime, Casey lies down to eat. He plops himself in front of his food, wraps his front legs around the dish, and nonchalantly partakes of his meal. Casey has never stood to eat. Neither does Casey run.

Rosalie's husband has tried time and again to take Casey jogging, but the golden retriever simply looks at his owner blandly. If anyone tries to coerce him into running, Casey staunchly resists going any faster than at a leisurely canter.

Casey is smart, obedient, and beautiful, but he can't go back to being a guide dog. And it's doubtful he'll ever learn how to eat standing up or how to run alongside his master. What's been done, is done.

Peter, who adamantly declared he would be true to the Lord Jesus even to death, denied him. John Mark, who was with the apostle Paul in the early days of ministry, deserted Paul and Barnabas in Pamphylia and didn't continue with them in their work (Acts 15:38). His action irreversibly fractured the missionary team. Although Jesus reinstated Peter into His service, and Paul later called for John Mark's help, no one could change the past. No one could undo what had been done.

It's often been said that God is the God of second chances.

It's often been said that God is the God of second chances. As well intentioned as the best of us are, we all fail. We fail God; we fail others. Circumstances or sin or any number of obstacles prevent us from following through on promises made. Similarly, others may disappoint us. But Jesus cautioned us, "Why do you look at the speck of sawdust in your brother's eye and pay no attention to the plank in your own eye?'" (Matthew 7:3).

Thank God that guide dogs don't have to be put down

secondary to someone's error in judgment. Thank God as He declares that "it is to [our] glory [that is, comeliness, honor] to overlook an offense" (Proverbs 19:11). Thank Him daily for His inexhaustible grace to us.

Discernment: Light versus Darkness

*Saints should be shedding light
exactly the way my collie sheds hair:
everywhere, all the time, in great
gobs from an endless supply
that can infuriate anybody who has
to deal with it clinging to them
whether they want it to or not!*

CHUCK MILLER

Marko

"Our God will fight for us!"
NEHEMIAH 4:20

Let me give it to you straight. We can do this one of two ways. You can cooperate, and you'll go to jail. Or you can put up a fight. If you do that, you won't fight me. You'll fight him, and you'll go to the hospital."

The apprehended suspect looked at the police officer; then he looked at "him"—a powerfully built, fawn-brown Belgian Malinois police dog named Marko. Nobody was smiling, including Marko.

The assailant opted for jail.

Brian is both a dog trainer and a police officer. Before he partnered with dogs in police work, he would frequently be involved in wrestling matches with suspects who resisted arrest. That all ended when dogs like Marko were added to the local law enforcement department.

Marko and other dogs like him are trained in tracking, patrol work, protection, and apprehension. They are also trained for use in narcotics, arson, and cadaver recovery. Like the officers they work with, dogs in law enforcement perform more than one task. They, too, have their good days and their bad days. Sometimes they get the bad guy. Sometimes they don't.

When Brian trained Marko, he didn't train him to be an aggressive or vicious dog. Marko was trained to do what comes naturally for him and for all dogs: play. Brian taught Marko to grab on to the prize—and hold on to it. When it comes to criminal apprehension, the name of the game for Marko is tug-of-war. Once the game is engaged, it's all or none.

Marko plays to win.

As Christians we have our share of wrestling matches. "For we wrestle not against flesh and blood, but against principalities, against powers, against the rulers of the darkness of this world" (Ephesians 6:12 KJV). We may fear being overpowered, but we are not alone in our struggles. We are commanded to "be strong in the Lord, and in the power of his might" (6:10 KJV).

> We are to resist attacks from the enemy prayerfully and practically.

When Nehemiah and the Israelites were rebuilding the walls of Jerusalem, they faced opposition. They met the challenge head-on in two ways: they prayed to God and posted a guard day and night to meet the threat. We are to resist attacks from the enemy prayerfully and practically.

Unbeknownst to Marko, he's not really involved in a playful game of tug-of-war but in a real war game. A game that has to do with law and lawlessness, right and wrong, life and death. Just as Marko holds on to win, so should we. "Fight the good fight of the faith. Take hold of the eternal life to which you were called" (1 Timothy 6:12).

David said, "If the LORD had not been on our side when men attacked us. . .they would have swallowed us alive." But he was able to go on and say, "Praise be to the LORD, who has not let us be torn by their teeth" (Psalm 124:2–3, 6).

It's just like Brian standing beside Marko—instead of in front of him.

Kaki

Crash! Bang! Clang! Thump!

Lisa jumped up from her chair when she heard the racket. She feared the worst. Her twelve-year-old cocker spaniel, Kaki, was in the area of the house from where all the noise emanated. Kaki has a long history of seizures. Lisa was sure this must be the most violent ever. She ran to the other room.

Kaki was not having a seizure, but she was very distraught. She had been having her usual nap right over one of the air-conditioning vents. When she got up, her dog tag caught in the grate. No matter what she did, that duct vent was attached to Kaki's collar. All the clanging, banging, thumps, and crashes would not free her from the metal albatross that clung to her. But the noise was just that: noise.

Relieved and laughing, Lisa released Kaki from her frightening but harmless noisemaker.

We are surrounded by noisemakers. Some, like Kaki's metal

grate, are harmless. Other noises are barely perceptible, yet dangerous—like the whispers and mutters mentioned in Isaiah 8 (above). Such sounds as these should be silenced by the words that give light.

Isaiah lived in the midst of great idolatry. He was the mouthpiece of God crying out to his people to turn to God for wisdom. "To the law and to the testimony!" he exclaimed. "If [the mediums and spiritists] do not speak according to this word, they have no light of dawn" (Isaiah 8:20).

No one—particularly one of God's people—is to consult mediums (psychics) or others purporting to commune with the dead or spirits. In desperation, King Saul sought a psychic for guidance when the Lord would not answer him. Saul only learned what he already knew: he had lost his kingdom. Defeat for him and his army was imminent.

The Lord calls psychic activity or fortune-telling defilement and prostitution. It is not harmless noise. Séances, levitation, Ouija boards, palm reading, the use of tarot cards—all such activity, done in relative noiselessness, is detestable to God (Deuteronomy 18:9–13). We need to protect our children from spiritism. We need to safeguard ourselves against it. We need to pray for friends who invite others over for an evening with a fortune-teller or palm reader. All such activity was a sinful practice in Moses' day, in Saul's day, and in the days of the apostles. It is sin in our day as well. God's final words of warning in Revelation are, "Those who practice magic arts. . .their place will be in the fiery lake of burning sulfur" (Revelation 21:8).

Sometimes the most alarming noises we hear are

> We need to be on our guard today and every day.

silly, easily corrected flukes. Sometimes the most subdued, hushed sounds are the most dangerous—and defiling—of all. We need to be on our guard today and every day.

Henry

*Jesus, knowing that they intended
to come and make him king by force,
withdrew again to a mountain by himself.*

JOHN 6:15

Gary describes Henry, his Jack Russell terrier, as a subway dog. From the time he was a young puppy, Henry has been riding the New York subway system. He travels everywhere with Gary. He's either in his specially designed duffel bag or alongside Gary on his leash. Henry has been a frequent flyer via all modes of public transportation: airliners, subways, and taxis.

Although Henry has been photographed numerous times (his bright red bandana makes him a picture-perfect model), Gary boasts of Henry's other qualities: he's gregarious, smart, and relentless.

On one particular trip, Henry was quick to greet everyone who took the time to give him a pat on the head or pet him. The crowds around him at the airport didn't intimidate him at all; he was ready to make friends. He was gregarious, just as Gary said.

But then Henry spied another dog across the airport terminal. Social hour was over. Henry went wild. He would not stop barking. He strained at his leash to keep the other dog in sight. Henry barked incessantly. Everyone in the airport found out just how relentlessly focused this gregarious little dog is. The swarming crowds of humans in no way distracted Henry from his focus: a nine-week-old puppy, comfortably snuggled in his own duffel bag, more than twenty-five feet away from him.

In some ways, Henry brings to mind the Lord Jesus Christ. Our Lord surely was gregarious when He walked the earth. He couldn't go anywhere without a crowd following Him. He called twelve men His friends. The Lord Jesus loves people, and He is loved in return. But while He was walking the earth, there were those who wanted to make Him the king by their own standards. Yet the Lord was not intimidated by their insistence (see John 6:15 above). He knew the way to kingship was by the cross. Through Isaiah, the Lord said, "Therefore have I set my face like flint, and I know I will not be put to shame" (Isaiah 50:7). Our Lord was relentless, focused in His pursuit of the prize: the redemption of people throughout all time—not just those who were alive during His earthly ministry.

> Our Lord surely was gregarious when He walked the earth. He couldn't go anywhere without a crowd following Him.

That same tenacity beat in Paul's heart. "Forgetting what is behind and straining toward what is ahead," he said, "I press on toward the goal to win the prize for which God has called me heavenward in Christ Jesus" (Philippians 3:13–14). Later, when his death was imminent, Paul wrote to his spiritual son, Timothy, "I have fought the good fight, I have finished the race, I have kept the faith" (2 Timothy 4:7).

Don't let the crowd intimidate you today. Heed the words of scripture to get a crown that will last forever by running life's race "in such a way as to get the prize" (1 Corinthians 9:24).

Red

*But there were also false prophets among the people,
just as there will be false teachers among you.
They will secretly introduce destructive heresies,
even denying the sovereign Lord who bought them—
bringing swift destruction on themselves.*

2 Peter 2:1

Eileen claims her dog was a religious canine.

This story took place a number of years ago when most people didn't consider dogs a nuisance. They enjoyed the run of their neighborhoods. Seldom were there stories of dogs attacking anyone. Dogs frequently chased cars, barked at the postman (all postal carriers were men back then), and played among the neighborhood children. Every dog was known by all the local residents who (as things were then) knew all their neighbors up, down, and on both sides of the street.

Red, whose name comes from his colorful, glossy coat, was unapologetic about where he chose to go. He liked to go where Eileen went and walked beside or just behind her with both pride and adoration. One of Red's favorite haunts was Eileen's church. When Eileen walked to church (few people drove to church back then), Red was not usually far behind. He waited outside until the service was over and then accompanied his mistress home. But once, Red's curiosity got the best of him.

Eileen was quietly listening to the sermon when she heard a small disturbance behind her. Then she heard giggles, then a small gasp and a whisper. Here came Red, sniffing his way along each pew until he located his mistress. With her face the color of her dog's coat, Eileen quickly exited the service with Red in gleeful pursuit.

Years ago someone said, "Going to church no more makes you a Christian than going into a garage makes you a car." How true that is. Yet we often assume because we see folks at church that they are a part of "the church of the firstborn" (Hebrews 12:23), as the Bible refers to true followers of Jesus Christ. Those outside the body of Christ also make the same erroneous assumption, much to the detriment of "the noble name of him to whom [we] belong" (James 2:7). We are encouraged to consider others better than ourselves, yet we are also cautioned to be as shrewd as snakes and as innocent as doves. In this context, shrewd means that we're to be prudent, sensible, and wise in relationships with others.

Just as in the days of the early church, there are those in the buildings we call our churches who are as yet outside the true church. Some of them are people truly seeking answers to life's tough questions. Some are curious. Some are ferocious wolves in the garb of sheep.

No one would mistake us for a dog if we were in a doghouse. No one mistook Red for a Christian in Eileen's

> Follow the advice of scripture. Train yourself to distinguish good from evil.

church. Don't be fooled by those who have "a form of godliness but [deny] its power" (2 Timothy 3:5). Follow the advice of scripture. Train yourself to distinguish good from evil.

Smokey

*"Look to the rock from which you were cut
and to the quarry from which you were hewn."*

ISAIAH 51:1

Ko more dogs."

That was Sandy's ultimatum to her husband. She and her husband had just gotten new flooring and new furniture. Her ultimatum had been forgotten. Not long after all the big purchases, Sandy came home from work to find her husband had gotten one more new thing: a dog.

Smokey, a sociable eighteen-month-old black cocker spaniel, had been purchased from a farmer. What the farmer neglected to tell Sandy's husband was that Smokey had never been inside anything except a barn in his life. When Sandy found Smokey, the newly redone living room had acquired a lived-in look in the worst sense of the word.

For two years Sandy and her husband tried to make Smokey into a house dog. Smokey was friendly, fun, and affectionate. But Smokey was an outdoor dog. He was used to roving, running, and romping with reckless abandon.

It's hard to romp with reckless abandon within the

confines of four walls.

Sandy and her husband took Smokey back to the farm. They opened the car door and turned him loose. Initially, Smokey tried to follow them—until he heard his mother's bark.

Smokey whirled around. He bounded toward the welcoming bark. He didn't look back.

When God spoke to his people through Isaiah, He told them to remember their roots. "Look to Abraham, your father, and to Sarah, who gave you birth," He said (Isaiah 51:2). God had done great things for the great patriarch of His people, and He promised to continue to do great things for them. Good roots and noble beginnings can suit us for continued blessing.

Bad roots can bring destruction. Through Peter, the Lord spoke of false teachers in the church. "If they have escaped the corruption of the world by knowing our Lord and Savior Jesus Christ and are again entangled in it and overcome, they are worse off at the end than they were at the beginning. It would have been better for them not to have known the way of righteousness, than to have known it and then to turn their backs on the sacred command that was passed on to them. Of them the proverbs are true: 'A dog returns to its vomit,' and, 'A sow that is washed goes back to her wallowing in the mud'" (2 Peter 2:20–22).

Smokey remembered the good things of his early life, but they did not equip him for the life of a homebound city dog. As people, we need to discern what in our past needs to be left behind and what needs to be retained. We are not to deliberately forget the truth God has given us; we are to live holy and godly lives.

Smokey quickly adjusted back to life on the farm. Proof again that we can take the dog out of the country, but we can't take the country out of the dog.

> We are not to deliberately forget the truth God has given us; we are to live holy and godly lives.

Ebony and Beethoven

What fellowship can light have with darkness?
2 CORINTHIANS 6:14

*D*on the teacher had a great idea for his class. He thought he would bring his dog, Ebony, and his yellow parakeet, Beethoven, to school. First, he would teach Ebony and Beethoven to do some tricks together. Thinking to first teach Beethoven to ride on Ebony's back, Don took Beethoven out of his cage and plopped him down next to Ebony, a cocker-poodle mix. Don did not know that, historically, both cocker spaniels and poodles have been bred as bird dogs.

A bright yellow bird perched on the back of a jet-black dog. The kids would love it!

Ebony and Beethoven sat on the floor quite companionably for a few seconds. Just how should Don begin?

Beethoven made a sudden movement. And just as suddenly. . .*chomp!*

Beethoven disappeared with a snap of Ebony's jaws. There was no way to tell that Beethoven had even been in the room—except for the bright yellow tail feathers sticking out beneath Ebony's black nose.

The bird was gone. The bird dog had done what his

ancestral lines had been bred to do.

The Lord warns Christians to "not be yoked together with unbelievers" (2 Corinthians 6:14). This word picture is from the Mosaic Law in which the Israelites were commanded not to yoke together two different kinds of animals. Different kinds cannot be appropriately yoked together—the results are disastrous. A donkey and an ox cannot plow a field together successfully. A godly man cannot be in business with a crook. A Christian young woman cannot enter into marriage with an atheistic man and hope that everything will work out.

Is it because God does not want us to influence others to become Christ followers? Is it because God has the best interests of some people at heart and not others? The answer to both questions is no. God is "not wanting anyone to perish, but everyone to come to repentance" (2 Peter 3:9). He sent His own Son not "to condemn the world, but to save the world through him" (John 3:17). There is not, has never been, and never be a man or woman on the earth whom God does not love. But God warns us not to yoke ourselves with those who do not share our love for the Lord Jesus Christ. It is for our spiritual well-being and lifelong benefit that God gives this command.

> There is not, has never been, and will never be a man or woman on the earth whom God does not love.

There is no harmony between Christ and the enemy of our souls, Satan.

One word emanated spontaneously from Don.

"Ebony!"

Ebony, true to his breeding, immediately dropped his quarry unharmed. There was not so much as a tooth mark on Beethoven. That was the last time Don tried to get a bird and a bird dog to perform as a team.

It's like trying to plow a field with a donkey and an ox yoked together.

A Future and a Hope

Yesterday I was a dog. Today I'm a dog.
Tomorrow I'll probably still be a dog.
Sigh! There's so little hope for
advancement.

SNOOPY

Laika

"You do not know when that time will come. . . .
If he comes suddenly, do not let him find you sleeping.
What I say to you, I say to everyone: 'Watch!' "
MARK 13:33, 36–37

Three-year-old Darl loved to go to Grandma and Grandpa's farm. He and Laika, his granddad's collie, were good friends. When Laika wasn't helping Grandpa with herding the cows, she was available for play. Laika, a spirited dog, had an ornery streak, however, and was often looking for a way to one-up the grandson who added a measure of fun to her workaday world on the farm.

Now a man, Darl remembers playing hide-and-seek with Laika. Darl would tear around the outside of the farmhouse to get away from Laika. He then enticed her to follow, calling out her name. After a few circles around the house, Laika figured out the game. Darl took off running. Instead of chasing him in hot pursuit, Laika took off the opposite way.

Wham!

Collie and boy collided—both running full bore— on the other side of the house. Darl was flipped up and over before he knew what hit him. Down but not hurt, he looked up at Laika who, Darl was quite sure, stood there with her tongue hanging out, her tail wagging, and a triumphant grin on her face. She raised her head imperially and trotted away.

Point. Game. Set.

> **As the coming of the Lord approaches, Jesus told us we are to be alert and wary.**

As the coming of the Lord approaches, Jesus told us we are to be alert and wary. "Be careful," He warned, "or your hearts will be weighed down with dissipation, drunkenness and the anxieties of life, and that day will close on you unexpectedly like a trap" (Luke 21:34). If we are careful to be rightly focused, that day won't be a trap to us. "Now, brothers, about times and dates we do not need to write to you," wrote Paul, "for you know very well that the day of the Lord will come like a thief in the night. While people are saying, 'Peace and safety,' destruction will come on them suddenly, as labor pains on a pregnant woman, and they will not escape. But you, brothers, are not in darkness so that this day should surprise you like a thief. You are all sons of the light and sons of the day. We do not belong to the night or to the darkness" (1 Thessalonians 5:1–5). Unlike Darl being blindsided by Laika, or unbelievers not understanding ahead of time what is happening, as obedient followers of the Lord Jesus Christ, we should be ready for—expecting—the Lord's return.

That day could be any day. Is your focus behind you, as Darl's was, watching for Laika? Or is it ahead and upward? Take to heart the words of our Lord Jesus: "Lift up your heads, because your redemption is drawing near" (Luke 21:28).

Roscoe, Tek, and Dozer

Let us hold unswervingly to the hope we profess,
for he who promised is faithful.
HEBREWS 10:23

$\mathcal{I}$t's a pit bull."

My eagerness to interview the young man who was carrying a small dog in a duffel bag vanished. A pit bull? I had never heard one good thing about pit bulls—or the people who own them. Better to let him and his dog go their own way. But I had to admit to some curiosity. My friend had spoken briefly to Michael, the man with the puppy asleep in his carry-on bag. I decided to learn a little something firsthand about pit bulls from Michael. Perhaps the media doesn't tell the whole story when it comes to pit bulls. I took a deep breath and walked over as casually as I could to the pit bull and his owner.

Michael was glad to talk to me about his dog. He has had three bull terriers (their proper name). Michael claims bull terriers are good with children, though they don't get along with other animals. Michael purchased Roscoe and his two previous bull terriers from breeders. He hopes

Roscoe turns out to be protective, but there's no guarantee he will. A bull terrier isn't automatically a fierce guard dog.

Michael hopes Roscoe, as he matures, will provide entertainment for the neighborhood children just as his predecessors, Tek and Dozer, did. Tek and Dozer had a favorite stunt. Michael would tie a rope to a tree and let one end simply dangle. Both dogs loved to jump up, clench the rope in their strong teeth, and hold on. Although the rope was a toy for swinging through the air, Tek and Dozer held on to it like Tarzan clutching a vine, swinging from tree to tree.

When a bull terrier holds on, he is epoxy with fur and a tail.

For us as Christians, there are things we are to hold on to as determinedly as Tek or Dozer hung on to their play rope.

"Hold fast to [the Lord] and. . .serve him with all your heart and all your soul," we're instructed (Joshua 22:5). We are strongly encouraged to "hold on to the good" in 1 Thessalonians 5:21. Like Timothy, we must take hold of the eternal life to which we have been called as believers (1 Timothy 6:12).

The writer of Hebrews tells us that we demonstrate the reality of our faith "if we hold on to our courage and the hope of which we boast" (Hebrews 3:6). We are further encouraged in the next chapter of Hebrews to "hold firmly to the faith we profess" (4:14).

An "hour of trial" (Revelation 3:10) is going to come upon the whole earth someday. As Christians we may already have hours of trial in a smaller, but just as real, sense. For those times, and for the prophesied future hour, the Lord Jesus encourages us. "I am coming soon," He says. "Hold on to what you have, so that no one will take your crown" (3:11).

> **Like a bull terrier, hold fast to the good.**

Like a bull terrier, hold fast to the good.

Cody

"For my thoughts are not your thoughts,
neither are your ways my ways,"
declares the LORD.

ISAIAH 55:8

*B*ob had a lot of work to get done. He let the dog out with him.

Cody, Bob's black Labrador retriever, has been his faithful pet for a number of years. Cody enjoys several activities, not the least of which is chasing rabbits—especially if the rabbits infringe on his home turf. On this day, Cody was content to sniff around the yard. Bob made fast work of the lawn, buzzing around on his riding mower.

Suddenly Cody started acting peculiarly. He kept getting in the path of the mower, preempting Bob's every move. The time came to do the final stretch of grass. Grumbling, Bob stopped the mower to get Cody out of the way.

To Bob's amazement, Cody showed him why he had been acting so strangely. Cody had been protecting a nest of baby bunnies. Bob picked up the nest, moved it out of harm's way, and climbed back on his mower. Content with his success, Cody went back to his own business. Bob finished the lawn.

So much in life cannot be explained or understood. Why should a dog who hunts rabbits suddenly decide to save some? By the same token, why does a consistently well-behaved dog suddenly viciously bite a child? Why do some animals parent a newborn animal of another kind while some animals devour or kill their own young?

When questions such as these involve human beings, the issues become even thornier and harder to comprehend. We question God's lack of intervention or His (apparent) acquiescence when terrible events besiege godly people or little children.

When Job and his associates tried to answer some of life's difficult questions, the Lord did not even begin to explain Himself. Rather, He answered questions with questions. "Where were you when I laid the earth's foundation?" He asked (Job 38:4). When a tower fell at Siloam, killing eighteen people, Jesus did not answer the unasked why. Rather, He asked, "Do you think they were more guilty than all the others living in Jerusalem? I tell you, no! But unless you repent, you too will all perish" (Luke 13:4–5).

We may not be able to answer life's small questions—why cats don't like mice or why a dog who hunts rabbits suddenly becomes a champion of bunnies. We certainly cannot answer the big ones—why a tower falls on an unsuspecting group of people or why a couple's only child is killed in an accident.

What we can know is that the Judge of all the earth will do right (see Genesis 18:25). We can know that

> We can anticipate that coming day with confidence and hope.

someday "the cow will feed with the bear, their young will lie down together" (Isaiah 11:7). Violence and calamity will cease forevermore.

Cody's rescue of a nest of rabbits is a faded, tattered, foretelling snapshot of the vibrant spectrum of tragedy-free life to come. We can anticipate that coming day with confidence and hope.

Maxx

Maxx waits eagerly at the door for his owner, Barb, to come home after working all day. He knows she probably has some leftovers from her lunch. He expects to devour the remaining tidbits within moments of her arrival. So he stands at the door, expectancy etched on every aspect of his thirty-three-pound frame.

Maxx is an unusual dog in a number of ways, aside from his dietary preferences. First, he is a tweener schnauzer. He's too small to be a standard schnauzer and too big to be a miniature. Maxx is also a true southpaw and not simply because he has paws and not hands. When he circles the floor to lie down, he circles to the left—never to the right. If he goes out to water the neighborhood trees and fire hydrants, he only raises his left leg. Maxx would never consider doing anything with his right paw. It's not in his personality. Finally, there is this issue of his unusual diet—the reason why he waits at the door whenever Barb goes to work.

Maxx loves very undoglike treats such as grapes, cauliflower, and carrots. Barb almost always takes raw produce in her lunch but seldom eats all of it—a fact Maxx counts on every day that Barb works. He can hardly contain himself when Barb comes in the door, her mostly empty lunch bag slung over her shoulder. Maxx is immediately beside her, poking about for the carrots he's waited for all day. (Carrots are his particular favorite.) His eager expectation is that his daylong wait won't be in vain.

Eager expectation. Do you recall the last time you were eagerly expecting something? Was it yesterday? Last week? Last year? Decades ago when you were a child?

Expectation brings visions of dancing about on nervous feet or eyes sparkling with anticipation. It is a word pregnant with hope, excitement, and reward. Its absence in our lives can make our daily existence dull, routine, and perhaps even depressing.

> Eager expectation. Do you recall the last time you were eagerly expecting something?

God tells us that the entire creation is waiting "in eager expectation for the sons of God to be revealed" (Romans 8:19). Why? Because frustration became our lot (and all of creation's) when sin spoiled God's perfect paradise. When the children of God are brought into glorious freedom, then the entire creation "will be liberated from its bondage to decay" (8:21). The completed redemption of all people will be the catalyst that frees the entire cosmos from entropy and decay. No wonder the creation is "groaning as in the pains of childbirth right up to the present time" (8:22). We are groaning as well, waiting "eagerly for our adoption as sons, the redemption of our bodies" (8:23).

If you're feeling hopeless today, consider these words: "There is surely a future hope for you, and your hope will not be cut off" (Proverbs 23:18).

It beats leftover carrots hands—and paws—down any day!

Dundee

And they admitted that they were aliens
and strangers on earth.
People who say such things show that
they are looking for a country of their own.
HEBREWS 11:13–14

When Tony and his wife were living in Tennessee, Tony rescued a poor, lost, brown-and-white Australian shepherd. Once he located his owners, Tony took Dundee back home. But twice a week for the next seven years, Dundee would show up at Tony's for a visit. He would come in and socialize with Tony and his wife then go back outside to sit on the front porch all night, standing guard.

Dundee loves herding and loves people. With a "go get 'em!" command, he would jump up, bark his loudest herding bark, and tear around the perimeter of Tony's house. Once. Then he returned right back to the front porch to gladly receive a pat on the head and words of praise for demonstrating his perfected herding skills.

As it turned out, however, Dundee was never lost in the first place. Tony's house was just one of a number of homes on his social circuit. He did similar things at the homes of others. One family regularly fed him hamburgers and let him watch television at their house. Dundee made the rounds every week, but he always returned home under his own power.

Unless, of course, a well-meaning stranger took the "poor, lost, brown-and-white Australian shepherd" home in his car.

There are some people similar to Dundee, who can make themselves at home anywhere. David and Becki, a missionary doctor and nurse serving in Gabon, are comfortable with rich and poor, educated and illiterate. They can live in the lap of luxury or in a simple hut. They take it in stride when performing surgery in a room without air-conditioning or modern, pristine equipment. They don't miss having a cell phone hanging on their hips 24/7. They are incredibly adaptable—and at home—living among an AIDS-ridden population and working in a third-world hospital.

Then there are those who never quite fit in anywhere. In chapter 11 of Hebrews we meet an assembly of people like this. The author says they are people who are "longing for a better country—a heavenly one" (verse 16). He includes famous people like Abraham and Moses. He lists people not so famous like Jephthah. Some are unnamed.

Whether we fall into the first group of people or the

> **Whether we fall into the first group of people or the second—or, what's most likely, somewhere in between—we can be confident in the Maker of all.**

second—or, what's most likely, somewhere in between—we can be confident in the Maker of all. He "fashioned and made the earth. . . to be inhabited" (Isaiah 45:18), but He has also prepared a place for us that we may be where He is (John 14:2–3).

Like Dundee, David, and Becki, we can be at home anywhere. Or, like Moses, we may always feel like an outsider. Either way, as Christ followers, no longer being at home in the body means we are in the "home of righteousness" (2 Peter 3:13).

Kuma

Now we see but a poor reflection as in a mirror;
then we shall see face to face.
Now I know in part;
then I shall know fully,
even as I am fully known.

1 Corinthians 13:12

There are some things that can be fully known about Kuma. She's a beautiful black Akita with some brindled markings and a super curly tail. Kuma is good with children and particularly likes toddlers. Kuma became fiercely protective when it was obvious her owner was expecting. Kuma loves ice cream and frozen yogurt; she's not particular about the flavor. When the nights are warm in northern Arizona, Kuma is ready and willing to lick the last spoonful of cold, sweetened delight off anyone's offered spoon.

Some mystery surrounds this ice cream–loving canine, too. How did she know her owner was carrying a child or that somehow she might, in some way, be more susceptible to harm and require increased vigilance? Now that Kuma's owner has had her new baby, she and her husband are waiting to see how Kuma will adjust to this new family member. Who knows how Kuma will respond when she has to share the last of some sweet treat with her usurper, Baby Shea?

When Kathy was a little girl, she was used to being the center of attention. Then her mommy went into the hospital and came out with a new baby girl. Without so much as a "Hi, Mommy" or any acknowledgment of her new sister, Kathy took one look at the infant and turned all of her attention back to her aunt, who was acting as taxi driver. "Can we go get some ice cream now, Aunt Esther?"

> There is no greater mystery than God the Son taking on human flesh to redeem us.

We never know just how pets or children will respond when a new family member arrives. It's a mystery. The Bible speaks of mysteries as well. "Beyond all question, the mystery of godliness is great," wrote Paul. "He appeared in a body, was vindicated by the Spirit, was seen by angels, was preached among the nations, was believed on in the world, was taken up in glory" (1 Timothy 3:16). There is no greater mystery than God the Son taking on human flesh to redeem us. Those living before Christ's coming could only try "to find out the time and circumstances to which the Spirit of Christ in them was pointing when he predicted the sufferings of Christ and the glories that would follow. . . . Even angels long to look into these things" (1 Peter 1:11–12).

We cannot know all things now. Much of this life—

not to mention the next—is a mystery. But we can trust Him whose knowledge is complete and for whom there is no mystery. We can rejoice that "God has chosen to make known among the Gentiles the glorious riches of this mystery, which is Christ in you, the hope of glory" (Colossians 1:27).

Coya

There [Jesus] was transfigured before them.
His face shone like the sun,
and his clothes became as white as the light.
MATTHEW 17:2

*A*re you sure that's not a coyote?"

The border guard was skeptical as he looked at Karen's orphaned puppy. The mangy, scrawny, woebegone animal had sidled up to her in Baja California, Mexico. Her pitiful condition and pitiable appearance tore at Karen's heart. She determined to adopt her and take her back home to Southern California, mange or no mange.

"I'm sure," she said. The locals in Baja had called Coya "little coyote" because that was exactly her appearance: big, pointed ears; a scraggly, lean body; and steely eyes. But Karen saw past all of that. She saw a pup who needed care. "She's a dog, all right," she reassured the officer for at least the third time.

The guard permitted her and Coya to enter.

On the long trip home, Coya was as still as stone. She lay in the truck with no interest in the passing scenery or where Karen might be taking her. She had found a friend; that's what mattered. For her part, Karen was taking Coya directly to a veterinarian who knew how to rid dogs of mange—and whatever else Coya might have. She knew her new pet would get top-notch care.

The dog Karen picked up some time later had undergone a transformation. Coya's coat was glistening with robust health. Her eyes were alert and sharp, and her disposition was one of uncontainable energy. She was almost out of control with her happiness. And it showed in every inch of her.

Peter, James, and John were privileged to see the Lord Jesus Christ transfigured before them. We get our word *metamorphosis* and its derivatives from the Greek word for "transfigure." Like the caterpillar that becomes

> We, too, will someday be transformed.

a butterfly, there was no resemblance between the Jesus whom the disciples walked with for three years and the Man who stood before them in that unique segment of time.

John later described Jesus as "a Lamb, looking as if it had been slain. . .[having] seven horns and seven eyes" (Revelation 5:6). When King Nebuchadnezzar saw the preincarnate Christ in the furnace of fire with Shadrach, Meshach, and Abednego, he could only stammer, "I see four men walking around in the fire, unbound and unharmed, and the fourth looks like a son of the gods" (Daniel 3:25).

We, too, will someday be transformed. "And just as we have borne the likeness of the earthly man, so shall we bear the likeness of the man from heaven" (1 Corinthians

15:49). "What we will be has not yet been made known. But we know that when he appears, we shall be like him, for we shall see him as he is" (1 John 3:2). The mange of sin will be gone forever. The natural body will be resurrected a spiritual one.

As Coya, our transformation will be complete. Like Christ, our transfiguration will be glorious!

Pursuit of God

*Let God's Word and God's love
be the herd dogs
chasing your thoughts into
the prayer corral.*

CHUCK MILLER

Buddy

Flee the evil desires of youth,
and pursue righteousness, faith, love and peace,
along with those who call on the Lord
out of a pure heart.

2 TIMOTHY 2:22

A horrible ruckus woke Barb and her husband from a sound sleep. Their sliding screen door was open. The awful noise continued from their backyard. Lights from their neighbors' adjacent houses started coming on.

What was all that racket?

Peering outside into the darkness, the couple saw movement. A bush in their backyard was. . .dancing. The small shrub was shaking, quivering, rustling, and alive with motion and noise. Guttural sounds emanated from the wildly waving bush. Then they saw it. Two glowing red eyes peeked from the heart of the vacillating shrub. They heard the deep-throated growl of their border collie, Buddy, who had opened the screen door.

With difficulty, Barb and her husband were able to get their single-minded dog out of the bush and back into the house. They then beat the bush (from a safe distance) in an attempt to scare out whatever it was that Buddy had trapped. A spiteful hiss came from the pointed snout of a frightened, angry opossum. Barb and her husband went back in the house to allow the scavenger a wide berth of escape.

From out of nowhere, Buddy burst on the scene again! Barking and running at the opossum with intensity and passion, his relentless pursuit of the invader was all consuming.

How in the world. . . ?

Once again, they dragged their reluctant pet back into the house. Barb feared Buddy would get rabies or worse from the clawed, sharply toothed scavenger.

Finally, the opossum escaped. The bush was again stationary, the night still. The neighbors' lights went off. Buddy quieted. After locking the screen door, Buddy's owners returned to bed, still wondering how Buddy got out the second time. They didn't have to wonder long.

They found a Buddy-sized hole chewed through their bedroom window screen.

In the last two letters written during his lifetime, the apostle Paul encouraged Timothy to pursue righteousness. *The Complete Word Study Dictionary* defines righteousness as "conformity to all that [God] commands or appoints. . .God's uprightness or standard." It is this righteousness that we are to pursue as hotly as Buddy pursued the opossum.

The Greek word used in the Timothy letters for "pursue" means "to follow or press hard after, to pursue with earnestness and diligence in order to obtain, to go after with the desire of obtaining" (*The Complete Word Study*

Dictionary). We are to pursue righteousness diligently. Those who "pursue righteousness" are to look to God whose "righteousness draws near speedily. . .will never fail. . . .[and] will last forever" (Isaiah 51:1, 5–6, 8). "The LORD. . .loves those who pursue righteousness" (Proverbs 15:9). It was for righteousness' sake Christ died. God made Christ "who had no sin to be sin for us, so that in him we might become the righteousness of God" (2 Corinthians 5:21).

> **We are to pursue righteousness diligently.**

To pursue righteousness with Buddy-like zeal is to find "life, prosperity and honor" (Proverbs 21:21). Righteousness is a worthy pursuit—with rewards lasting beyond a bush-beleaguered victory.

Reba

Her one white paw makes her stand out. Reba is a small shepherd-collie mix. Her brown eyebrows and snout—and that singular white paw—constitute her unique markings. Reba has another unique peculiarity.

Reba loves to go backpacking with her owner, Alycia. Alycia stuffs her backpack with everything she needs in the wilderness—bedroll, food, and water. Reba carries her own supply of water and dog food in the saddlebags draped over her sides. She is free to walk, climb, or run, just like her owner. Reba is an adventuresome free spirit, even if she's small. Reba likes to encourage this same free-spiritedness in others.

Alycia was in her apartment one afternoon when she heard a shrieking commotion outside. She went to the window to investigate and saw two very angry crows. They were dive-bombing something on the ground. Cawing and squawking, they dove toward the ground repeatedly, their sharp beaks like drawn weapons. Alycia paled. *Reba!*

Alycia ran outdoors, fearful that the crazed crows were attacking her dog. The reason for the hullabaloo became immediately clear. Reba was following a baby crow who had no more interest in flying. The baby bird was oblivious to its frantic parents. Reba, meanwhile, was focused on encouraging the baby bird to fly. Reba was heedless of the hysterical bigger crows, too. She just kept gently prodding the young crow along with her nose. The pattern was the same:

Nudge. . .hop. . .nudge. . .hop. . .nudge. . .hop.

Reba's well-meaning encouragement was wasted on the fledgling bird that kept focused on the ground beneath him instead of the sky above. Reba's same, well-intentioned encouragement was completely misunderstood by the panicked parents overhead.

Those whose intention it is to encourage others are often misunderstood. Sometimes these encouragers are perceived as an irritating nuisance. Occasionally they are ignored. Sometimes, however, they are seen as a threat.

Christy grew up in an unchurched family. She came to know the Lord as a teenager. Not long after that, she was called by God to become a missionary. Her family was dumbfounded.

She wanted to do what? She wanted to go where? Christy's parents were neither supportive nor encouraging. Like the parent crows, they thought only they knew the way Christy should take. Others were encouraging her in this?

Though Christians in general and Christian missionaries

in particular suffered persecution in the early church, missionaries Silas and Judas "said much to encourage and strengthen the brothers" (Acts 15:32). Paul, who suffered grievously as a missionary, still encouraged the second-generation missionary, Timothy, to preach the Word. No matter how difficult the challenge, Paul never told Timothy to turn back from his calling.

> Whether you are a parent crow or a nudging encourager, be careful to spur on any aspiring missionary to fly to foreign lands.

Whether you are a parent crow or a nudging encourager, be careful to spur on any aspiring missionary to fly to foreign lands. It matches the beat of God's missionary heart.

ANOTHER Bailey

Taste and see that the LORD is good.
PSALM 34:8

Bailey, a West Highland white terrier, has expensive tastes. Bailey turns up his nose at dog food. But restaurant food is food he can really sink his teeth into! His owner, Sherri, has been known to make a quick trip to a local restaurant when she didn't have anything suitable for this finicky Westie. Bailey has been known to eat dog food out of a dog dish under duress, but he makes no bones about his dissatisfaction. But Bailey's tastes exceed fast-food fare.

Bailey likes to eat the mail as well. Not junk mail—never junk mail. He in no way helps rid the house of unwanted advertisements or credit card promos. Bailey rather prefers to chew up the newest edition of *Sports Illustrated* or, during one of his more recent and costly meals, a United States savings bond. The savings bond incident almost relegated Bailey to dog food for the rest of his life.

Fortunately for Sherri and for Bailey, Sherri was able to gather up what saliva-soaked chunks were left. She mailed them back with an explanation. Uncle Sam was able to decipher enough of the dog-eared bond to reissue another one to Sherri.

Sherri was able to tuck away her new savings bond in a safe place. Bailey was—temporarily at least—out of the doghouse.

> Do you have an insatiable taste for the words of the Lord?

Do you have an insatiable taste for the words of the Lord? The psalmist said, "How sweet are your words to my taste, sweeter than honey to my mouth!" (Psalm 119:103). Peter said that once we have tasted that the Lord is good, we ought to crave spiritual nourishment "so that by it [we] may grow up in [our] salvation" (1 Peter 2:2–3).

The Lord Jesus Christ said to Satan, "Man does not live on bread alone, but on every word that comes from the mouth of God" (Matthew 4:4). Just as Bailey has craved more than dog food in his life, our tastes need to go beyond daily physical nourishment.

When the Lord Jesus spoke the words above to Satan, He was quoting from the Old Testament. The context of that verse makes it clear that there was a lesson associated with God's provision of sustenance. "Remember how the Lord your God led you all the way in the desert these forty years.... He humbled you, causing you to hunger and then feeding you with manna, which neither you nor your fathers had known, to teach you that man does not live on bread alone but on every word that comes from the mouth of the Lord" (Deuteronomy 8:2–3).

When you sit down for lunch today, reflect on your

taste—your craving—for the words of God. Consider seriously the prophecy of Amos: " 'The days are coming,' declares the Sovereign LORD, 'when I will send a famine through the land—not a famine of food or a thirst for water, but a famine of hearing the words of the LORD' " (Amos 8:11).

New Dog

These are the twelve he appointed:
Simon (to whom he gave the name Peter).
MARK 3:16

ylvia's new dog was a beagle-Lab mix. She and her family went through the usual process to train their new dog. They were pleased to find he learned quickly. Then the day came when the new dog had to be left home alone. Sylvia and her husband took the new dog upstairs and closed him inside the bathroom. They assumed that was a good spot—no worries about him getting into the garbage or anything like that.

On their way out to the grocery store, they left a note for their son. "The dog's in the bathroom. Let him out when you get home."

When Sylvia was in aisle three, her cell phone rang.

"Hey, Mom! The dog's here in the living room," her son said. "I thought you put him in the bathroom."

"We did!"

"Well, he's down here now. Everything seems okay. I just thought it was weird that he met me in the kitchen when you left this note saying he was upstairs."

"Hmm. I'm sure we closed the door tightly." Sylvia looked at her husband, who shrugged his shoulders. "Oh well, we'll be home soon." She flipped her phone shut and dropped it back in her purse.

In aisle four, the phone rang again.

"Hey, Mom! Did Dad put a big hole in the bathroom door for some reason?"

In American culture we seldom change our first names. Nor do we give our children names to make a statement. God did it with Abram. Ruth's mother-in-law, Naomi, did it with her own name. But the closest we usually come to a purposeful name change is simply adopting a nickname.

This was not the case for Sohn and Gmlee, a poor couple who live in Cambodia. When their third son was born, they named him Gamsought—*pitiful*. Their lives were hopelessly pitiful "without hope and without God in the world" (Ephesians 2:12). The present was joyless and their future hopeless. According to their beliefs, they must have been wicked in their previous lives. Now they were paying their dues.

But Sohn and Gmlee saw a change in their neighbors, who were just as poor as they. They smiled. They were kind; they were joyful. Although the other young family's condition was as pitiful as theirs, they were living as if they had hope.

Through the influence and intercession of those newly born-again neighbors, Sohn and Gmlee became Christ followers themselves. Their poverty remains unchanged, but Sohn and Gmlee now have Christ in them, "the hope of glory" (Colossians 1:27).

They told their missionary pastor, "We don't want to call

our son Gamsought anymore. His name is Yoseph." Yoseph means "God will add."

How blessed the hope that is Christ!

> How blessed the hope that is Christ!

Names are important. And in case you're wondering, Sylvia and her family did name their new dog before he ate his way out of the bathroom.

His name is Woody.

Jiggs

"Do you not say,
'Four months more and then the harvest'?
I tell you, open your eyes and look at the fields!
They are ripe for harvest."

JOHN 4:35

Jiggs started life as the toy collie no one wanted—except Les. Leslie's neighbor came over with his puppy.

"You want a dog?" he asked. "I don't want to keep this dog anymore."

Les's wife shook her head. They had had one dog that gave them nothing but trouble. She didn't want another.

"Sure. I'll take him," Les said. Jiggs had the peach-fuzziest coat he'd ever seen on a puppy.

"Outside," his wife said. "The dog stays outside."

Jiggs settled in, and soon the family didn't remember how life was before Jiggs came. Playful but well behaved, he was soon everybody's favorite. When winter came, Leslie's wife couldn't bear to see their silky collie outside. Jiggs moved in.

Les has a habit of looking out the front window at least once a day. He gets up from his chair or the sofa, walks to the window, and watches the comings and goings of people across the street at the local bowling alley. Les grew up and now lives and works in his small town. If he's not at the bowling alley bowling in his own league, he looks out the window to see who else frequents his favorite spot.

Every evening Les goes to the window. Every evening Jiggs follows him. Les looks out, and Jiggs does, too. He puts his paws up on the windowsill, looks at his master's face, and then fixes his eyes on the exact same spot as Les. The routine is the same day after day, year after year. Every so often, Jiggs momentarily looks back up at Les, but he turns his gaze back to the building across the street. He remains steadfast at the window, looking out the same as his master.

Jiggs wants to see life through his master's eyes.

As the disciples looked on the fields, they saw the future harvest. The Lord saw the fields as people and said the harvesting, the gathering of people to their Creator, was long overdue (John 4:35). When the disciples looked at a huge crowd, they said, "Where could we get enough bread in this remote place to feed such a crowd?" (Matthew 15:33). When Jesus looked at the same crowd, He said, "I have compassion for these people" (15:32).

When people brought children to Jesus to be blessed, the disciples rebuked them. Indignant, Jesus rebuked the disciples and "took the children in his arms, put his hands on them and blessed them" (Mark 10:13–16).

When Jesus and His disciples were exiting the temple in Jerusalem, "one of his disciples said to him, 'Look,

Teacher! What massive stones! What magnificent buildings!' "What the Lord saw was destruction coming (Mark 13:1–2). It took the disciples a long time to see people and things the way their Master did.

> Will we look at life today with the same compassionate intensity of our Master?

And us? Will we look at life today with the same compassionate intensity of our Master?

Grateful

One of [the lepers], when he saw he was healed,
came back, praising God in a loud voice.
He threw himself at Jesus' feet and thanked him—
and he was a Samaritan.

LUKE 17:15–16

Al was enjoying a leisurely walk in the forested hills around the Japanese countryside. He and his wife were visiting his wife's family in Japan. Al loves the outdoors and spends as much time as he can exploring any regions that are new or unknown to him. He heard a dog yelping and carrying on, but he didn't see one anywhere in his immediate vicinity. He continued on his way back to his in-laws, though he remained bothered by the crying and yelping he heard.

"You did the right thing," his wife told him when he returned to the house. "It would be considered interfering if you poked your nose into someone else's business. This is Japan—not the United States. People mind their own business here. They expect you to do the same."

Al deferred to his wife's advice for a while. Being a dog owner himself, however, he wasn't convinced that there wasn't some trouble. He had heard desperation in the barking.

He couldn't stand it. He went back to investigate.

When Al came to the area where he had first heard the yelping, there was silence. He stopped and listened, but there was no sound. Still, he went a little farther away from the woods and back toward the homesites. Then he found him.

A black Labrador puppy hung dangling from a fence. His leash had caught. He was hanging unconscious and unmoving. Al groaned and ran to the little dog. He was sure the dog was dead; he looked lifeless. Al untangled the breathless little body from the leash that had become a noose. He gently laid the flaccid pup down on the ground.

Suddenly, the puppy took a quivering, gulping gasp of air. He was alive!

For the next ten minutes, Al was lathered in the jubilant kisses of the once-again breathing, living Labrador puppy.

Thankfulness can be expressed in so many ways, yet often there is a sorry lack of it. In the account of the Lord's healing of ten lepers, He was amazed that only one out of the ten returned to give praise to God. Throughout the Word, we are encouraged to be thankful people. "Give thanks to him and praise his name," we're told, "for

> **Throughout the Word, we are encouraged to be thankful people.**

the Lord is good" (Psalm 100:4–5). "Sing to the Lord with thanksgiving" says the psalmist (147:7). Our prayers and petitions are to be studded with thanksgiving as well.

A spirit of thankfulness sets us apart from those who, in the last days, are described as "lovers of themselves" and "ungrateful" (2 Timothy 3:2). We, by contrast, are to be "overflowing with thankfulness" (Colossians 2:7).

Live thankfully today. Just like that one returning leper. Just like the kiss-crazy, six-week-old puppy. Just like the puppy's owner, whose effusive thanks said he was glad the American tourist interfered.

Duchess and Duke

Remember your Creator in the days of your youth.
ECCLESIASTES 12:1

Duchess, an eight-month-old Labrador pup, finds life to be one exciting adventure after another. Her favorite pastime is taking a ride in the car. When Joy, her owner, is ready to go somewhere and invites Duchess along, Duchess is at the door. When the door opens, she bounds outside in wild anticipation. She jumps up and into the car. Duchess doesn't wait for an open car door; she flies through the open window! She plops herself down in the passenger seat, parks one paw on the window ledge, and is ready to go cruising.

Duke, Joy's other Labrador, does not get excited about rides. To be honest, he doesn't get excited about much of anything. He never runs to the car. He'd never consider leaping through an open window. Duke has been around the block a few times. He's older, wiser. He prefers to sit at home and enjoy the quiet—without boisterous Duchess.

Duchess adores the older Labrador. She is under his nose, in his way, and always wanting to romp with him. She loves him like he's her daddy. At the end of her busy days, Duchess curls up next to Duke and snuggles in contentedly.

Duke tolerates Duchess and her adoration. He doesn't snap or growl at her; he languidly endures her constant motion and attention. He resigns himself to her closeness when she cuddles up to him at night, but as soon as Duchess falls asleep, Duke beats a hasty retreat.

Duke enjoys a more settled life.

Josh comes from a loving, godly home, but he's young and passionate about evangelism. During summers while in college, Josh went south, not homeward and north. Beach evangelism consumed one summer; evangelism and discipleship filled another. Once he finished school, Josh went to the Netherlands for a year's service, training others in campus ministry. He came home for a couple of weeks to pack for his next summer project: evangelism and making of disciples in Macedonia. Josh has the youth, the stamina, and the passion to tackle great things for Christ's kingdom.

> There is great encouragement in the scriptures for the younger generation.

There is great encouragement in the scriptures for the younger generation. "Don't let anyone look down on you because you are young," wrote Paul, "but set an example for the believers" in everything (1 Timothy 4:12). John the apostle said he was writing to the overcoming young men of the church because "you are strong, and the word of God lives in you" (1 John 2:13–14). Even in the Bible's oldest book, we're told, "It is not only the old who are wise, not only the aged who understand what is right" (Job 32:9).

If you have the vigor of Duchess, be ready to spring through the open window God provides! "The harvest is plentiful but the workers are few" (Matthew 9:37).

Mister B

*"Set apart for me Barnabas and Saul
for the work to which I have called them."*
ACTS 13:2

Troy and his family were worried about Mister B, their
black-and-white border collie. A nearby skeet shoot had
scared him, and he had run off, terror-stricken. They
searched the area for Mister B, but he was nowhere to be
found. It was winter. The temperature that night dropped
below freezing. Still no Mister B.

Two days passed. Three days.

Troy printed flyers and posted them in a large radius.
Troy was afraid that Mister B would freeze to death in the
elements. He played outside daily, but he was their house
dog, unaccustomed to life in the wild. Another day passed.
Still no Mister B.

Then the telephone messages started.

Beep! "We saw your dog eating our cat's food."

Beep! "You the folks with the missing dog? We think
we saw him chasing a train."

Beep! "We spotted your dog in our yard."

Beep! "We saw your dog chasing our dog!"

But with all the Mister B sightings, no one could ever
catch him. Troy and his family would drive to the areas

from where the calls came, only to return empty-handed. After Mister B had been gone six days, Troy gave up hope of ever finding their dog.

On day seven, Troy got a call from the local dog pound. Mister B was there, ready to be taken home. Troy expected to find Mister B wasted and worn from his ordeal in the elements, but when he arrived to pick him up, Mister B was as hale and hearty as he'd ever been.

Mister B had had the time of his life!

Jon was mauled in an African river by a hippopotamus. His recovery was slow, but he continues to live and work in Africa twenty years later.

Jeff and Jo were held up at gunpoint in broad daylight, but they didn't pack their bags and leave Brazil forever. They made it through the frightening flashbacks and still minister in Brazil.

Living in Buenos Aires, Mary invites a group of working moms over for coffee, Bible study, and fellowship each week. She is the only nonsmoker in the thick haze created by her chattering, laughing, chain-smoking companions. Yet every week she marvels at the passion her new friends are developing for the Word of God.

In spite of each of these stressful, hurtful events, each of these missionaries will tell you they are "having the time of their lives." They take seriously the call of God to "make disciples of all nations" (Matthew 28:19), and that's what they're doing. Like Paul, they are compelled by the Spirit to do what they do in an attempt to reach others with the gospel of Jesus Christ. What looks like suicide to others is

> **Jon, Jeff, Jo, and Mary are out to take the world for Christ. Are we?**

what Paul calls The high calling of God in Christ Jesus" (Philippians 3:14 KJV).

Mister B was out to take the world by storm.

Jon, Jeff, Jo, and Mary are out to take the world for Christ. Are we?

Boch

So I turned my mind to understand,
to investigate and to search out wisdom
and the scheme of things.
ECCLESIASTES 7:25

*B*och, a black-and-gold German shepherd, was born in Czechoslovakia. This German-Czech dog now makes his home in the United States and has a varied, interesting career. When he's not doing public relations work among young schoolchildren, Boch is in law enforcement as a police narcotics dog.

John, the detective Boch works with, suggests no one enjoys his work more than Boch. When it's time to go on a drug search, it's off to the races for Boch. He is eager to get into the car and go to work. Most of their work is done in houses, searching for illegal narcotics. John, armed with a search warrant, and Boch, equipped with his super sniffer, search every room thoroughly. Sometimes their work takes them outside. Boch puts his nose to work sniffing around, under, and in vehicles. Sadly, Boch and John are invited into schools occasionally for locker sniffs. In every case, Boch's sense of smell is this team's primary weapon in the war on drugs.

How exactly was Boch trained for this kind of police

work? Narc dogs are taught that narcotics discovery is a game. The toy, the prize, the reward is the illicit drug. When it's time to sniff his way around a house, a school, or a vehicle, Boch considers his duty nothing more than a big game—a game he is out to win for the sheer fun of discovery!

John says Boch finds drugs in places he would never even think to look, like under the base molding below a kitchen sink. Boch is out to win every game he plays. He searches with meticulous diligence and tenacity. His reward is in the discovery.

Solomon said he gave his life to the study of wisdom. "To search out a matter is the glory of kings" is a proverb he wrote (Proverbs 25:2). He may have had the Persian king Xerxes in mind when he penned those words. King Xerxes had a niggling suspicion that he had overlooked something important earlier in his reign. By searching it out, he discovered his gross omission and made amends that very day. Xerxes got out of bed and took the time to carefully search out a matter (Esther 6).

> To understand God's ways, we need to apply ourselves to the scriptures.

Luke, the writer of Acts, commended the Berean Jews because they searched the scriptures daily (Acts 17:11). The Lord Jesus told the skeptics around Him to search the scriptures because they testify about Him (John 5:39).

To understand God's ways, we need to apply ourselves

to the scriptures. Peter said that "the prophets. . .searched intently and with the greatest care" to learn of the coming Christ (1 Peter 1:10–11). We can do no less since the holy scriptures are able to make us "wise for salvation through faith in Christ Jesus" (2 Timothy 3:15).

Like Boch searching out the world's tainted treasure, we are to search out true treasure. We need to get *our* noses into a good book—the Good Book.

Death and Resurrection

My collie, myself:
created for the wilds,
bred for home.

CHUCK MILLER

Blarney Stone

They stoned Paul and dragged him outside the city,
thinking he was dead.
But after the disciples had gathered around him,
he got up and went back into the city.
Acts 14:19–20

Blarney Stone was one tough dog. As a farm dog, he was protector, playmate, guard, and intimidator all rolled into one. Blarney was a dependable snake killer. Although he was playmate and babysitter for Bob's kids, Blarney would dispose of cats as zealously as he did snakes. When thieves broke into Bob's garage, Blarney sounded the alarm. Blarney performed all his duties around the farm with temerity and resilience. But the most remarkable thing about Blarney Stone was his near indestructibility.

Blarney had a bald spot from an inadvertent scalding, but he made a full recovery. He ran full bore into a chain-link fence several times and never got so much as a minor head injury. He pursued a cat up to the second story of a house. When the cat jumped to the safety of a tree, Blarney fell to the concrete below. He got up, only slightly stunned, and lived to pursue another cat another day. Blarney was hit by a snowmobile, too—more than once.

The most graphic demonstration of Blarney's mettle

came the day Bob accidentally ran over him. Bob was driving the tractor after a prolonged rainstorm. Blarney came from out of nowhere and dodged under the tractor. Bob looked back and saw Blarney, smashed deep into the mud. Bob parked the tractor. With heavy steps, he went back to get Blarney to bury him. But Blarney was gone. He'd run off; he had other things to do.

Blarney had the proverbial nine lives of a cat.

"Five times I received from the Jews the forty lashes minus one. Three times I was beaten with rods, once I was stoned, three times I was shipwrecked, I spent a night and a day in the open sea.... I have known hunger and thirst and have often gone without food; I have been cold and naked. . . . [I] was caught up to the third heaven. Whether it was in the body or out of the body I do not know—God knows" (2 Corinthians 11:24–25, 27; 12:2). This is how the apostle Paul describes part of his life. When on the island of Malta, he suffered no ill effects from a viper's venomous bite. It must have appeared to others that Paul was indestructible.

> The important question remains then: What do we do with the days or years God gives us?

Some of us may be like Blarney and Paul and defeat death time and time again. But "man is destined to die once, and after that to face judgment" (Hebrews 9:27). The important question remains then: What do we do with the days or years God gives us?

You may have to pull yourself up out of the mud today—or shake off a viper of past venomous hurts. In either case, echo the words of the psalmist who prayed, "Teach us to number our days aright, that we may gain a heart of wisdom" (Psalm 90:12).

ANOTHER BOOTS

"I the LORD do not change."
MALACHI 3:6

Boots is a mature dog of sundry breeds. She knows what she likes, and what she doesn't like: change. Boots has her favorite place at the front window. She likes to jump up on the chair and watch for the approach of friends or callers. When Sally, her owner, rearranges the furniture, Boots makes her indignation known. She stands at the spot where the chair is supposed to be and gives Sally disgusted looks. Boots does not like change in her environment.

Boots does not like change when it comes to those who come calling. She has her favorite people among her owners' friends and family. Her most favorite person of all is Kenny; he has animal magnetism. There's hardly an animal—especially any dog—that Kenny has yet to meet and not like. Pets have always taken to Kenny like. . .well, like fleas to a dog. Boots is no exception. She loves her Kenny devotedly. When he and his wife come for a visit, Boots is ecstatic. From the time Kenny enters the house, Boots never leaves his side. She likes nothing better than to sit beside (or on) Kenny and let him pet her. Kenny likes nothing better than stroking Boots's soft fur when he visits. For years there was never a change in this familiar, happy pattern.

Then Kenny went home to be with the Lord.

The first several times Kenny's wife went to her brother and sister-in-law's house, Boots barely greeted Betty. After Betty came in, Boots kept watching the door for Kenny. Then she went over to the window and put her paws up on the windowsill, looking out. Then she went back to the door. Then back to the window. No Kenny. This was one change Boots had never anticipated—and one she did not like. No matter how long she peered out the window, Kenny never came. Death had changed Boots's happiest times forever. And as Betty said in watching Boots: "I know just how Boots feels."

> **Change demands adaptation, reorganization, prioritization, and. . . more change.**

Most of us don't like change. It is not always something as drastic as death that brings change. Change may come on the heels of a new career, a new school, or a doctor's diagnosis. Whatever heralds a change—good or bad—we are generally resistant to it. Change demands adaptation, reorganization, prioritization, and. . .more change.

Knowing all this, isn't it wonderful to know God doesn't change? Samuel told King Saul, "He who is the Glory of Israel does not lie or change his mind; for he is not a man, that he should change his mind" (1 Samuel 15:29). God "does not change like shifting shadows" (James 1:17).

"Jesus Christ is the same yesterday and today and forever" (Hebrews 13:8).

Dreading the next change to come in your life? Take the hand of the Changeless One. Praise Him with the writer of the Book of Hebrews. "But you [Lord] remain the same, and your years will never end" (1:12).

Trajan

*"I will repay you for the years
the locusts have eaten."*
JOEL 2:25

This dog was nothing like the dog she had lost to death the previous month.

MaryBeth's first dog was a female blond cocker with almost no tail, a blunted nose, and soft, floppy ears. This mixed-breed dog was a black-and-white male with a curly tail and pointed ears. The young dog looked nervous in the cage of his temporary residence. He regarded his potential owner with timid curiosity.

"He is house-trained," the woman said. "He understands, knows, and obeys commands."

MaryBeth wanted a new pet. The house was too quiet without the *tap-tap-tap* of doggy feet echoing on the floors since her beloved Buffy had died. She made her decision. She named her new dog Trajan and took him home.

MaryBeth first took Trajan around the perimeter of the yard. He sniffed about happily, eagerly.

Then the two of them went into the house. Like Buffy, Trajan would be a house pet. MaryBeth removed the leash.

Trajan took off!

First, he bolted into the living room and ripped down

some drapes. (He did not heed any commands to stop or come.) Next, he tore into the kitchen where he brazenly emptied his bladder on the kitchen wall. MaryBeth had no time to reprimand him. He ran full tilt back into the other room! There he proceeded to finish his elimination process on the floor.

MaryBeth was stunned. They had not been in the house five minutes.

What could she do? MaryBeth sat down on the floor, dissolving into tears. Her previous dog had never done anything like this. Memories of her buff-colored cocker came flooding back.

"You are not Buffy!" she cried. "You are not!" Sorrow for her loss swelled over MaryBeth again.

Immediately Trajan came to her. He gently licked her tear-streaked face as if to say, "I'm sorry."

From that moment forward, Trajan has been an obedient, loving, well-behaved dog. MaryBeth once again hears the happy *tap-tap-tap* of doggy feet in her empty-no-longer house.

Death changes things. Death never comes at a good time. God has made us to know intrinsically that death is not the way things are supposed to be. God has "set eternity in the hearts of men" is how scripture says it (Ecclesiastes 3:11). Death is a distortion; it is not "natural." At Lazarus's grave, the Lord Jesus "was deeply moved in spirit and troubled" (John 11:33). The Lord was about to raise Lazarus from the grave, yet He Himself was disquieted. Death was never what the Creator had in mind or heart for His creation.

But sin came. Death, of necessity, followed.

But not for long.

Jesus Christ has defeated death. It "has been swallowed up in victory" (1 Corinthians 15:54).

> **Jesus Christ has defeated death.**

Soon "there will be no more death. . .the old order of things" will pass away (Revelation 21:4)!

Tipper

[Christ] shared in [our] humanity
so that by his death he might destroy him
who holds the power of death. . .
and free those who all their lives were held
in slavery by their fear of death.
HEBREWS 2:14–15

*I*f you ever want to meet a friendly dog, Tipper is the dog for you. He would never win Best of Show, even if he did try his paw at canine competition, but he excels in what counts: affection and good humor. Tipper is of the opinion that everyone should be as lovingly affectionate as he is, though he is sometimes rebuffed by those who do not share his joie de vivre. Tipper sets about to give his sloppy doggy kisses to anyone and everyone. (He is no more a good watchdog than a show dog.)

There is one subtle fray, however, in the usual happy-go-lucky fabric of Tipper's sanguine disposition. On regular occasions, Tipper's good humor dissipates like early morning fog in the warm sunlight. Tipper is afraid—deathly afraid—of thunder. No matter how his owner tries to console him, Tipper is inconsolable. No amount of rhythmic stroking or gentle cooing can release Tipper from his stranglehold of fear.

Do you have a fear like Tipper's? Have you an unrelenting, persistent fear that few, if any, know about? Does a singular, paralyzing fear lurk just behind your usual good humor?

Do you fear getting cancer? Never having a child? Do you fear losing your lifelong mate—or pet? Do you fear speaking in front of a crowd? Are you afraid your son will get into drugs, or that your teenage daughter will become pregnant? Afraid that you'll not be able to make your next house payment?

Do you fear getting old? Not getting old? Death?

Do you fear life?

We all have fears. Things that—reasonable or not, significant or not, real or imagined—hold us in slavery. Have you ever noticed how often the Lord says, "Do not fear," in the scriptures?

When an angel of the Lord appeared to the lowly shepherds, did he say, "Isn't this great? You're seeing a bona fide angel!" Hardly. These shepherds, used to fighting off wild animals and robbers with crude, simple instruments, were ready to bolt. The angel had to say, "Do not be afraid" (Luke 2:9–10). When the Lord Jesus Christ walked on water, He had to say, "It is I. Don't be afraid" (Matthew 14:27). On his way to Jairus's house to resurrect the ruler's daughter, He said, "Don't be afraid; just believe" (Luke 8:50).

> **Fear not. Don't be afraid.**

Fear not. Don't be afraid. The Lord understands our death fear—death of health, death of esteem, death of companionship. All our lives we can be held captive by it—until we grab hold of the One who defeated death by His own death and resurrection.

Feeling like Tipper today? Hearing the roll of thunder? Hold on to Him who gives peace in the storm. Hold on to the One who "has compassion on those who fear him" (Psalm 103:13).

Bernard and Siblings

"You hurled me into the deep,
into the very heart of the seas,
and the currents swirled about me;
all your waves and breakers swept over me."

JONAH 2:3

*S*he heard the puppies whimpering in the middle of the night.

Kathy rolled over with a yawn. She was sure Mama boxer would take care of her six whimpering puppies, including the runt of the litter, Bernard.

But the whimpering and crying continued. Kathy groaned when she looked at the clock, but she got out of bed to investigate. She went downstairs. Lady Samantha, the puppies' mother, appeared oblivious to the cries of her brood. Kathy glanced outside.

It's raining cats and dogs, she thought to herself with another yawn. She flipped on the light switch and plodded down the basement steps. She couldn't believe what she saw.

There were Bernard and all his siblings, doggy-paddling for everything they were worth. The basement had flooded; their wire cage was a watery prison. The pups were wide-eyed with fear, paddling and barely keeping their heads above water. Kathy yelled for her husband.

"Get something to put the puppies in!" she told him. She waded through the water to rescue the four-week-old pups.

Kathy's husband ran to get the first thing that came to mind. He ran out into the downpour. He hoisted up the kids' plastic swimming pool, dumping all the water onto the saturated ground. He squeezed the pool through the doorway and plopped it down on the kitchen floor.

Kathy placed the dripping-wet pups into the plastic shell. Bernard and all the other baby boxers were saved from drowning—with a swimming pool.

> God's means of rescue aren't always what we expect.

Rescue doesn't always come in the form or manner we expect. As Jonah was about to drown, he cried out to the Lord. Little did he expect to be delivered by a huge fish. "But the LORD provided a great fish to swallow Jonah" (Jonah 1:17), and Jonah was saved.

King Darius was outwitted by some of his political appointees. Consequently, he had to throw his trusted adviser, Daniel, to the lions—literally. The king spent a miserable, sleepless night as he awaited morning. Daniel's triumphant words to the king the next morning were, "O king, live forever! My God sent his angel, and he shut the mouths of the lions. They have not hurt me" (Daniel 6:21–22).

God's means of rescue aren't always what we expect.

Sometimes they aren't what we want. He may use death to rescue some. "Devout men are taken away, and no one understands that the righteous are taken away to be spared from evil" (Isaiah 57:1). Those words are hard, yet they can comfort us in times of loss.

Who would think that a swimming pool would save puppies from drowning?

That a fish would deliver a man from turbulent seas?

That God can use the last enemy—death—against itself (1 Corinthians 15:26)?

Rest today knowing that, even if His means are unconventional, God is our great Deliverer (Psalm 18:2).

Duke

Duke is a big, imposing golden retriever who catches the attention of people when he's out and about with his master. But Duke isn't just another pretty face or a show dog. He's a well-seasoned, well-traveled assistance dog.

Tyler, his owner, had extensive surgery for a brain tumor years ago. Although Tyler survived both the tumor and the surgery, complications left him with multiple disabilities. His equilibrium was most severely affected, relegating him to life in a wheelchair.

Until Duke came along.

With Duke at his side to steady his gait, Tyler has been empowered to do the things he loves and visit the places he wants to go. Duke was the first assistance dog permitted into the Hawaiian Islands without a layover in quarantine. Duke has been up the ski slopes via a gondola and down to the Cayman Islands swimming with Tyler and the stingrays. Duke has been to eight major-league baseball stadiums and to almost every Toledo Mud Hens home game.

Because of some disfigurement from his tumor and

subsequent surgery, Tyler used to draw the stares of some people. Now the focus of strangers is on rock-steady Duke. The question most asked of Tyler is "Can I pet your dog?"

When Moses was elderly and could no longer lead his people in battle, he held up his hands to God. But weariness overtook him even then; he had to depend on Aaron and Hur to hold "his hands up—one on one side, one on the other—so that his hands remained steady till sunset"

> When it's in our power to do so, we must be ready to help restore equilibrium for those who are struggling emotionally or physically.

(Exodus 17:12). Moses, the man of God, had come to a time in life when he depended on others for steadiness.

There may be occasions today when we will have to mimic Hur and Aaron. We may be called upon to steady another. "Help the weak," God tells us (1 Thessalonians 5:14). "Strengthen the feeble hands, steady the knees that give way" (Isaiah 35:3). When it's in our power to do so, we must be ready to help restore equilibrium for those who are struggling emotionally or physically.

Or, like Moses, we may need the steadying influence or support of another. If and when that time comes, we need to graciously and thankfully receive the assistance of others.

But what if no one comes to our aid? What if we're left to flounder alone? What then?

Even if we do not have a dependable dog like Duke or one earthly friend who loves us at all times, we have the promise of the Lord God, who will never leave our side. "Even to your old age and gray hairs I am he, I am he who will sustain you. I have made you and I will carry you; I will sustain you and I will rescue you" (Isaiah 46:4).

Sophie

"This sickness will not end in death."

JOHN 11:4

Jodi's puppy, Sophie, became critically ill when she was five months old. The Pembroke Welsh corgi, with her squat legs and large, at-attention ears, was listless and dreadfully sick. Jodi took Sophie to her veterinarian, hopeful that he would be able to diagnose and treat whatever was ailing the ill pup.

Sophie had a stuffy nose, diarrhea, vomiting, and a high fever. The vet gave Sophie fluids and sent her home with Jodi. Still, Sophie continued to deteriorate. She was returned to the vet's where, in spite of IVs, she developed seizures and only got worse. The vet recommended euthanasia.

Jodi was torn. She didn't want Sophie to continue suffering, but at the same time, the dog was so young. Her life had barely begun—and now they were going to end it? Jodi and her husband struggled with their decision, but finally, they decided to take Sophie home. They would nurse her, try to keep her from suffering, and simply love her until she breathed her last breath.

For weeks Sophie continued in her netherworld of grave illness. Jodi did what she could, hoping against hope to get Sophie through her sickness. The vet again recommended euthanasia. He was convinced Sophie would not—could not—survive. But Jodi continued with her loving nursing care.

One day Sophie showed interest in cottage cheese. Jodi bought a big container of it, but Sophie wouldn't eat any more. The next day she munched on some bologna. Jodi was ecstatic! She gave Sophie as much as she wanted. This was how her feedings continued for the next few weeks: Sophie showing temporary interest in a variety of bizarre foods but eating them and keeping them down.

Jodi watched with delight as, day by day, Sophie slowly got better. The vet was speechless.

Jesus' disciples must have been more than stunned when they arrived in Bethany to find that their Lord's dear friend Lazarus had died. The Lord had told them he wouldn't die. Jesus was so confident about this He had stayed where He was two more days (see John 11).

When Lazarus's sisters greeted Jesus, they both said, "Lord, if you had been here, my brother would not have died" (John 11:21, 32). To His disciples, the Lord said, "[Lazarus's sickness] is for God's glory so that God's Son may be glorified through it" (11:4). To Martha He said, "He who believes in me will live, even though he dies" (11:25).

Sometimes God does the miraculous via an incontestable miracle. Sometimes He accomplishes the miraculous through the gentle ministrations of loving human hands or through persistent prayer or both. God is God in all. He is not limited in how He does His work—no matter anyone's skeptical unbelief.

You can ask Jodi, who now has a normal, healthy, adult Welsh corgi named Sophie.

Someday you can ask Lazarus—and others—who still live in spite of all earthly evidence to the contrary.

> God is God in all.

Penny

Listen, I tell you a mystery:
We will not all sleep, but we will all be changed.
1 Corinthians 15:51

The dreaded moment had come.

It was time to put their dog to sleep. Penny had been the family's only dog for over ten years. Her naturally wavy black fur was now studded with gray. Her floppy ears looked the same, but they didn't hear as well as they once did. Lately she was having difficulty getting around. Her two back legs had trouble keeping up with the two in front. Ken and his wife decided euthanasia was best for their little dog. The kids were grown, they themselves were gone a lot, and it was just as well for Penny, who now spent most of her days napping.

His wife watched as Ken picked up their chubby, graying little mutt and carried her out the front door. Her husband got as far as the front steps and came back in.

"I can't do it," he said.

In spite of her growing deafness and impaired mobility, Penny gave them another year of sweet companionship before she died.

Jimmy told his Sunday school teacher, Roseanne, that his

parents had put their dog to sleep.

"They said she was old. We had to put her to sleep, and she went to heaven."

Roseanne gave Jimmy her condolences at his loss. *He's so young to have to grapple with the harsh reality of death.*

"How old are you, Teacher?" he asked after a brief pause.

Roseanne was surprised by Jimmy's sudden change of subject, but she smiled and answered him. "I'm thirty-seven," she replied.

Jimmy's eyes got wide. "Oh boy," he remarked. "You'll be going to heaven soon, too!"

Do you find it as puzzling as I do that we still speak of sleep when discussing the demise of our animals, but we seldom speak so euphemistically of our own dying? Sometimes the Lord Jesus spoke of death as sleep. When pressed, Jesus did not say that death was a type of soul sleep but a reality. Death grieves the heart of God; it wasn't His original intent for us.

> The Lord Jesus Christ, God incarnate, has triumphed over death.

Whatever word or phrase we might use for death does not change its harsh actuality. But death is not the final word. The Lord Jesus Christ, God incarnate, has triumphed over death. Resurrection, rising from the dead, waking from sleep—all these terms show that death is not the end. Jesus' victory over death is unrivaled. "I am the First and the Last. I am the Living One; I was dead, and behold I am alive for ever and ever!" (Revelation 1:17–18).

As believers in our Lord Jesus Christ, we shall share in His life. The picture given us is one of unsurpassed triumph. "The throne of God and of the Lamb will be in the city, and his servants will serve him. They will see his face, and his name will be on their foreheads. . . . And they will reign for ever and ever" (Revelation 22:3–5).

Bibliography

Jensen, Irving L. *Jensen's Survey of the Old Testament.* Chicago: Moody Press, 1978.

Pfeiffer, Charles F., and Everett F. Harrison, eds. *The Wycliffe Bible Commentary.* Chicago: Moody Press, 1962.

Scofield, C. I., ed. *Oxford NIV Scofield Study Bible.* New York: Oxford University Press, 1984.

Strong, James. *Strong's Exhaustive Concordance of the Bible.* Iowa Falls, IA: Riverside Book and Bible House.

Zodhiates, Spiros, ed. *The Complete Word Study Dictionary: New Testament.* Chattanooga: AMG Publishers, 1992.